The Cambridge Introduction to
Marcel Proust

Proust's *A la recherche du temps perdu* (*In Search of Lost Time*, 1913–27) changed the course of modern narrative fiction. This *Introduction* provides an account of Proust's life, the socio-historical and cultural contexts of his work and an assessment of his early works. At its core is a volume-by-volume study of *A la recherche*, which attends to its remarkable superstructure as well as to individual images and the intricacies of Proust's finely stitched prose. The book reaches beyond stale commonplaces of madeleines and memory, alerting readers to Proust's verbal virtuosity, his preoccupations with the fleeting and the unforeseeable, with desire, jealousy and the nature of reality. Lively, informative chapters on Proust criticism and the work's afterlives in contemporary culture provide a multitude of paths to follow; the book charges readers with the energy and confidence to move beyond anecdote and hearsay and to read Proust's novel for themselves.

ADAM WATT is Senior Lecturer in French at Royal Holloway, University of London. He is the author of *Reading in Proust's* A la recherche: *'le délire de la lecture'* (2009), and editor of *Le Temps retrouvé Eighty Years After/80 ans après: Critical Essays/Essais critiques* (2009).

The Cambridge Introduction to
Marcel Proust

ADAM WATT

Royal Holloway, University of London

CAMBRIDGE UNIVERSITY PRESS
Cambridge, New York, Melbourne, Madrid, Cape Town,
Singapore, São Paulo, Delhi, Tokyo, Mexico City

Cambridge University Press
The Edinburgh Building, Cambridge CB2 8RU, UK

Published in the United States of America by Cambridge University Press, New York

www.cambridge.org
Information on this title: www.cambridge.org/9780521734325

First published 2011

Printed in the United Kingdom at the University Press, Cambridge

A catalogue record for this publication is available from the British Library

Library of Congress Cataloguing in Publication data
Watt, Adam A. (Adam Andrew), 1979–
    The Cambridge Introduction to Marcel Proust / Adam Watt.
      p.   cm
    ISBN 978-0-521-51643-3 – ISBN 978-0-521-73432-5 (pbk.)
    1. Proust, Marcel, 1871–1922–Criticism and interpretation.   2. Proust, Marcel,
    1871–1922. À la recherche du temps perdu.   I. Title.
    PQ2631.R63Z9817 2011
    843′.912–dc22
    2010052338

ISBN 978-0-521-51643-3 Hardback
ISBN 978-0-521-73432-5 Paperback

For Stace
Mon amour, ma chérie

Contents

Texts and abbreviations

All quotations are taken from the Vintage Classics edition of *In Search of Lost Time* in six volumes, translated by C. K. Scott Moncrieff (except for *Time Regained*, translated by Andreas Mayor and Terence Kilmartin), revised by Terence Kilmartin and D. J. Enright (Vintage, 2000–2). Page references are also provided to the single-volume 'Quarto Gallimard' edition of *A la recherche du temps perdu* which, although it does not have the admirable critical apparatus of Jean-Yves Tadié's four authoritative *Pléiade* volumes (Gallimard, 1987–9), reproduces the same text in handle-able and considerably more affordable format. The following abbreviated forms are incorporated in the text (the roman numerals refer to the Vintage volume numbers):

I	SW	*Swann's Way*	SW	*Du côté de chez Swann*
II	BG	*Within a Budding Grove*	JF	*A l'ombre des jeunes filles en fleurs*
III	G	*The Guermantes Way*	G	*Le Côté de Guermantes*
IV	SG	*Sodom and Gomorrah*	SG	*Sodome et Gomorrhe*
V	C	*The Captive*	P	*La Prisonnière*
	F	*The Fugitive*	AD	*Albertine disparue*
VI	TR	*Time Regained*	TR	*Le Temps retrouvé*

Where the abbreviated form is the same for both English and French texts, it only figures once, the English page number preceding the French. I have at times modified the Vintage translation (indicated by 'trans. mod.' in the text). References to Proust's essays and shorter writings are taken from *Against Sainte-Beuve and Other Essays*, translated by John Sturrock (Penguin, 1988) and *Contre Sainte Beuve précédé de Pastiches et mélanges et suivi de Essais et articles*, ed. by Pierre Clarac and Yves Sandre (Gallimard, 1971) and are incorporated in the text in the form *ASB* or *CSB*, each followed by page numbers.

All references to Proust's correspondence (abbreviated to '*Corr.*', followed by a volume number and page reference) are to the *Correspondance de Marcel Proust*, ed. Philip Kolb, 21 vols. (Plon, 1970–93); translations from the correspondence, and from all other works in French, unless otherwise stated, are my own.

Introduction

By anyone's standards, Proust's *A la recherche du temps perdu* (*In Search of Lost Time*, 1913–27) is a very long book: seven novels combine into a single overarching narrative, whose multiple strands keep even the most committed readers occupied for months, even years. *Time*, therefore, is an integral part of the enterprise. The story is relatively simple: an individual narrates his life in the first person, seeking to determine what it amounts to and whether he has it in him to become a writer. To read the novel, however, involves relearning our experience of time, not only in the novel's radically unconventional structuring but in its themes and the ways in which it takes over our empty minutes, fills our cramped commuter journeys and our soaks in the bathtub with expansiveness and capaciousness previously unknown in literature. A single evening party stretches out to fill scores of pages; and the fleeting real-time duration of sensations – a smell, a sound – are drawn out and intensified by the onward rush of prose that seeks tirelessly to capture every conceivable contour of human experience. This is not time wasted. It is time revitalized or, rather, it is the novel sensitizing us to literary time and, through this, to a store of experiential riches in the real world that might otherwise pass us by.

The novel's original translator, C. K. Scott Moncrieff, rendered Proust's title as *Remembrance of Things Past*, a phrase borrowed from Shakespeare's Sonnet 30, which begins 'When to the sessions of sweet silent thought/I summon up remembrance of things past'. Moncrieff's title is often still heard, but the voluntary, willed nature of 'summoning' runs counter to the importance granted by Proust to *involuntary* memory; 'Remembrance of Things Past' also loses the original balance between the 'temps perdu' (lost time) of the overall title and the 'temps retrouvé' (time regained) of the final volume. *In Search of Lost Time* was adopted as the novel's English title in 1992 when D. J. Enright revised Terence Kilmartin's 1981 revision of Moncrieff's translation. The *Search*, however, was not Proust's only work. Interested readers can dip their toes, even immerse themselves, in his early writings if they are so minded: the results are mixed, but the overall impression we come away with is that of a writer gradually honing a voice, refining his material and seeking a form that will let one express the other. Proust's generic experimentation was vitally instructive and the hybridity of his efforts in the determining year between 1908 and 1909 – pastiches, essay, dialogue, novelistic fragments, theoretical reflections on art – was never wholly eradicated from the *magnum opus*, whose corrections were still unfinished when its author wheezed his last shallow breath in 1922.

The *Search* is perhaps the greatest achievement of twentieth-century literary modernity, an improbable feat of individual creativity. It incorporates numerous traits of style and technique of nineteenth-century literature: romantic reflection and self-absorption; realistic accounts of people, places and events; naturalistic studies of genealogy and vice. It also takes in a vast sweep of history and culture, from cave paintings to Carpaccio, Mozart to music hall, Napoleon to Nietzsche and Nijinski, Leonardo to Lloyd George, Socrates to Sévigné. Proust's penchant for Russian doll-like clausal constructions, sentences that sprawl unhurriedly over several pages, sets him apart from his immediate forebears, yet his equally frequent habit of formulating laws and maxims puts one in mind of the seventeenth-century *moralistes* La Bruyère and La Rochefoucauld.

This remarkable stylistic palate and expansive range come to us from a narrator who turns his gaze outwards to the proliferating multiplicities of the material world but just as often looks inwards, at times with increased intensity, at the tensions and traumas, real and imagined, of his own subjectivity. A large measure of Proust's radical modernity stems from the non-linear unfolding of the novel. Prolepsis (anticipation) and analepsis (flashback) are narrative devices familiar to us in film and fiction nowadays but Proust was among the first to use them systematically in structuring a literary work. Using them, as well as subtle, sometimes unmarked shifts in perspective (movements between the Narrator's older and younger selves) in a novel as expansive as the *Search* tests readers to their limits and foregrounds the importance – and the fallibility – of memory, the mental faculty Proust prizes above all else. The result is a reading experience unlike any other in the Western tradition.

Most famously, near the start of the novel the Narrator's childhood, long thought to be a forgotten, and therefore inaccessible, chapter of his past, is recaptured for him as an adult when he tastes a *madeleine*, a small, sweet cake, dipped in lime-blossom tea. This sense experience, far more powerful than any willed act of the mind, revitalizes involuntarily the experience of tasting the same concoction as a child; this memory opens the floodgates and a crucial period of his existence is vividly restored to him.

Also key in the Proustian world are the complex workings of habit. Habit can dampen our senses to the stimuli of the outside world, cocoon us in an environment that is anodyne, in*habit*able. For Proust's Narrator, an absence of habit brings with it anxiety, uncertainty and fear. Coming to terms with a new environment (such as an unfamiliar room in which he must sleep) requires the Narrator to re-establish from first principles his identity and his relation to the world at large. While with time habit anaesthetizes the hyper-sensitive Narrator to the fears by which he is assailed, a routine existence shaped solely by habit (like that of Aunt Léonie in Combray) is one which threatens to limit his experience of the world and the things in it to a purely superficial level, dictating patterns of behaviour that curtail spontaneity and opportunities for real discovery. As a result the Narrator treads a treacherous path between his fear of being damaged by a complex, threatening world and his unparalleled thirst for knowledge. Whether we seek knowledge of a sonata or a salon, of how our lover finds his or her pleasure or, harder still, of his or her intimate thoughts and desires, we run the risk of ridicule by revealing our ignorance, our vice or our obsession. Worse, we might discover truths we are not equipped to handle, knowledge that with enlightenment brings suffering.

The conception of love and relationships that emerges from the *Search* is a pessimistic one. The Other is unknowable; what we call 'love' is a projection that comes from the self and whose reflection we mistake for reciprocal affection. Desire is all-powerful until the object of desire is possessed; then 'love' withers, our interest diminishing directly as intimacy with the Other increases. Although in the novel satisfaction from relationships is scant and suffering in love is the lot of individuals of every social station, there is in the many of the novel's lovers the same streak of resilience and tenacity that we find in Vladimir and Estragon in Beckett's *Waiting for Godot*, that keeps the embers of optimism aglow: against the odds they go on in the hope that happiness, or at least a cessation of suffering, may yet be near at hand.

The Narrator's compulsive knowledge-seeking together with his fear of the unknown combine to produce one of literature's most engaging and at times infuriating monologists. His urge to understand states of mind, impressions and sensations makes the *Search* a remarkable *roman d'analyse* or psychological novel, a sustained, rhapsodic study in interiority. Yet the Narrator's quest is not only for his own identity and vocation. He seeks an understanding of art, sexuality and worldly and political affairs: he is a snoop and a voyeur; he comments and classifies; his taxonomic impulse makes the novel appear to be a vast compendium, replete with burrowing wasps and bedsteads, military strategies, stereoscopes, asparagus and aeroplanes. The metaphors and analogies the Narrator persistently uses act as conduits between the realms of mind and matter and remind us of the fluidity of their boundaries for the creative artist.

Proust's Narrator is at times an incisive thinker, a virtuoso splitter of intellectual hairs and an accomplished cartographer of the human heart and mind. Frequently, however, his greatest insights come from fumblings in the dark, wrong turns and contingent revelations. He swings between confidence and neurosis, is a dupe and an ignorer of good advice, often because of the blinding force of jealousy. He is a sensitive aesthete seeking affection and happiness who sequesters his beloved and slowly suffocates her with a brutal regime of surveillance and interrogation.

With the caveat that an *Introduction* can never be a substitute for the labour of reading and rereading Proust's work itself, what follows offers a crutch for the weary and a set of access routes for those setting out on the journey for the first time. *In Search of Lost Time* is a unique achievement and reading it is a life-changing process. The novel explores the ragged, shifting nature of subjectivity; it abounds in beauty, intelligence, cruelty and suffering. It is hoped that this volume will stimulate the readerly appetite of those jaded or misled by the much-peddled '*madeleine*-induced bliss', 'cork-lined room' conceptions of Proust and his work. This *Introduction* reminds readers that Proust's novel offers sustenance far longer-lasting, richer and more nourishing than cork or crumbs.

Chapter 1

Life

Proust led an almost irresistibly intriguing life. It was one of wretched ill health combined with seemingly endless creative stamina; desire in surfeit but scant satisfaction; wealth and privilege coupled with perennial yearnings for the company and favours of those of a lower social station. These aspects of the life make for fascinating reading and can feed profitably into our understanding and appreciation of Proust's novel, but if we tarry too long over them we risk becoming bewitched by the man and his manias, losing sight of the art to which he dedicated his life.

As biographers and critics have profitably shown for decades, Proust drew on practically every aspect of his personal experience when creating his novel. His life and the rapidly changing world in which he lived provided inspiration, ideas and scenarios, which fed into the construction of his literary project. But this, crucially, does not mean that Proust and his Narrator are one and the same. Proust had a brother, a Jewish mother, a sinecure position for a time at the *Bibliothèque mazarine*; the Narrator of the *Search* has none of these. Proust was homosexual; for his heterosexual Narrator, lesbianism is a threatening, unknowable otherness that provokes in him pathological fear.

Detailing such divergences, however, is something of a fool's errand. For every aspect of the Narrator we consider that sets him apart from his creator, another will present itself that suggests congruity or sameness. Some readers (and critics of the novel) think of the Narrator as 'Marcel', a choice which implicitly aligns the Narrator's identity with that of his creator and asks a brief moment of the novel to bear a great deal of critical weight. In *The Captive* (which Proust had not finished editing when he died) the Narrator remarks that Albertine, awakening, would 'say "My – " or "My darling – " followed by my first name, which, if we give the narrator the same name as the author of this book, would be "My Marcel," or "My darling Marcel"', (*C*, 77; *P*, 1658). This sudden acknowledgement of the Narrator's fictional status and that of the text in which he appears introduces a bewildering ontological dilemma for readers to ponder but is not iron-clad 'proof' that the novel's protagonist *is* 'Marcel' and less still that being so named would mean that he and Proust are one and the same person.

Matters are complicated by the fact that in his correspondence and the notes made during the writing of the novel, Proust habitually adopted the first person when referring to the Narrator of his novel, thus blurring the line between creator and created. Additionally, George Painter, Proust's first, highly influential, English-language biographer, worked on the premise that the *Search* was a 'creative autobiography'. Understanding the novel, for Painter, was largely a question of mapping Proust's fictional characters on to his real-life acquaintances. Taking all these matters into account, it is most straightforward, and it will be my practice in the present volume, to refer to the individual who leads us through the pages of the *Search* simply as the 'Narrator', similar to but separate from the work's author.

I shall discuss Proust's life not because the information thus imparted provides a necessary foundation upon which to rest one's reading of the *Search*, or because knowing which individuals from Proust's social circle may offer 'keys' to certain characters will make the novel easier to comprehend and enjoy. Rather, it is fruitful to begin with a consideration of Proust's life because an awareness of his family background, his health and upbringing, the relations he developed through childhood into adolescence and his conduct in the affairs of his adult life can provide us with a valuable sense of the forces that shaped this singularly complex individual. Readers whose primary interest is in Proust's novel should inform themselves of biographical fact and anecdote in the way that we might visit a vineyard in order to note how the breeze comes down the slopes, to see how the sun strikes the grapes and to feel the texture of the soil between our fingers, fingers that later will hold a glass of something quite distinct but inextricably related to that earlier experience.

The image of Proust that one might gather from journalistic references is that of a bedridden hypochondriac, a hyper-sensitive, moustachioed aesthete, notoriously nocturnal, independently wealthy and idiosyncratic in taste. There is, naturally, factual foundation for these enduring images: his biographers offer accounts of the treatments he took for his asthma, the installation of the cork lining on the walls of his bedroom, the unusual hours he kept, the drinks and dishes he favoured; and the photographs we have of him at different ages will permit those so minded to piece together a rough timeline for the growth and development of the famous moustache. The clichéd conceptions of Proust, however, which lodge in the collective imagination a picture of an author familiar even to those who have not read his work, are based largely on our knowledge of the adult Proust. What of his childhood and adolescence? Perhaps we should start there if we are to gain some sense of the child that would be father to this most exceptional man.

Proust was born on 10 July 1871 in Auteuil, a village to the west of Paris where his mother's uncle had a house to which his parents had moved when the disruption and violence of the Paris Commune grew intolerable. He was a weak baby and the family harboured serious doubts about his chances of survival. When he was well enough they moved back to Paris. Their vacations were spent largely in Illiers, the paternal family seat to the south-west of Paris, near Chartres. Proust would later draw heavily on the landscapes and way of life at Illiers in constructing the 'Combray' section of *In Search of Lost Time*. In 1971, to mark the centenary of the author's birth, the village's name was formally changed to Illiers-Combray; it continues to attract a great many Proustian pilgrims. Proust's mother, born Jeanne Weil, came from a wealthy Jewish family (her grandfather made his fortune in porcelain manufacture and her father was a stockbroker) and his father, Adrien Proust, was Catholic, although neither practised their respective religion. Proust was baptized and confirmed in the Catholic Church and he and his brother Robert, born in May 1873, were raised as Catholics.

Proust's initial weakness and poor health are one explanation for the strong bond he developed with his mother. His relationship with her was closer than that with his father, in large part because of the latter's career. Adrien Proust was a successful doctor, held in high public regard, who published extensively on a wide range of subjects of medical science. His implementation of the use of the '*cordon sanitaire*' or quarantine line in the fight against cholera contributed to his election to the prestigious *Académie de médecine* in 1879; by 1885 he was elected Professor of Hygiene in the Faculty of Medicine. He travelled a lot, worked long hours and believed in the benefits of regular exercise and the strict scientific treatment of illness. As his career went from strength to strength his first son's health gradually deteriorated.

In the spring of 1881, returning with his parents from a walk in the Bois de Boulogne, Marcel had a sudden choking fit: this asthmatic seizure that almost killed him marked the beginning of his lifelong struggle for breath and inaugurated what would thereafter be a constant nervous fear of the open air and an extreme sensitivity to dust, pollen and smoke. After the onset of his asthma, longer spells were spent on the Normandy coast, where Adrien believed the sea air would have a beneficial effect on his son's respiratory problems.

Proust attended the Lycée Condorcet in Paris from 1882 until 1889 but missed a great deal of schooling for health reasons. At this time it was popular for children to have keepsake books, albums which included questionnaires friends filled out so as to learn more about each other. Proust completed one such questionnaire in 1886: judging by his responses, the adolescent Proust was romantic, idealistic and had pastimes befitting his age, health and upper-middle-class background (favourite occupations: 'Reading, day-dreaming, poetry, history, theatre'). About six years later Proust took a similar questionnaire and his answers are revealing of his development. He was extremely fond at this time of Marie de Benardaky, a girl with whom he played in the gardens of the Champs-Élysées, and Jeanne Pouquet, the companion of Gaston, son of Mme Arman de Caillavet, a society hostess whose salon Proust had recently begun to frequent. It is at Pouquet's feet that Proust can be seen strumming a tennis racket-guitar, mock serenading her in a well-known photograph from 1891 or 1892. Despite his attraction to Pouquet and other young women in the late 1880s, tellingly, in the second questionnaire, Proust described his favourite quality in a man as 'feminine charm', his favourite qualities in a woman as 'Manly virtue and openness in friendship'. These answers anticipate his later challenging of commonplace conceptions of gender identities in his novel.[1]

Letters from the late 1880s offer evidence of Proust's sexual experimentation with his (all male) classmates at Condorcet. But his inquisitiveness was more than libidinal. From a young age he read widely; at the Lycée he read set texts such as Pascal's *Pensées* and Leibniz's *Monadology* as well as recent and contemporary writers such as Barrès, Renan, Leconte de Lisle and Loti. He began contributing to journals run by his classmates, amongst whom were Daniel Halévy, who became a noted historian and biographer; Fernand Gregh, later a major critic and member of the *Académie française*; and Robert de Flers, another future *Académicien*. As well as drawing on his reading and the intellectual and amorous stimulation he received from this remarkable peer group, Proust's perspective on the world also developed through his precocious participation in the salon life of *belle époque* Paris. He was an enthusiastic reader of Anatole France and it was in the salon of Mme de Caillavet, France's mistress, that Proust eventually met the eminent writer who, in due course, provided the preface for his first book, published in 1896, the year France was elected to the *Académie française*.

Proust's health was still precarious and he harboured desires to become a writer, so his decision in 1889 to sign up voluntarily for military service upon graduating from the Lycée may seem surprising. It was in fact calculated: those *volunteering* undertook just one year's service rather than being enlisted for the normal three. The young intellectual was stationed to Orléans, but his asthma disrupted his fellow cadets so he was lodged privately in the town (which now has its rue Marcel Proust). Early on in his service, in January 1890, Proust's maternal grandmother, Adèle Weil, died from an attack of uraemia. Proust's mother, devastated, went into mourning, travelling later in the year to Cabourg where previously they had holidayed, the three generations together;

there she sought consolation in reading the letters of Mme de Sévigné, her mother's favourite author. Proust returned to Paris after his military service with thoughts of becoming a writer, but with little sense of how he might do so. His parents wished him to study with a view to a stable future (of the sort that writing could not guarantee), so, somewhat reluctantly, in November 1890, Proust enrolled in the Faculties of Law and Political Science, the conventional pathway for those seeking a diplomatic career.

His studies were a minor part of his existence, however, as writing of a number of non-academic sorts began to occupy him: he wrote for *Le Mensuel*, commenting on societal and political affairs, and founded, with a group of ex-Condorcet students, *Le Banquet* (the title borrowed from the French rendering of Plato's *Symposium*), a journal in which he published reviews and sketches based on his ever-growing experiences in the salons. It was at this time that Jacques-Émile Blanche (1861–1942), an established society painter, began his sketches and eventually completed the portrait by which Proust's youthful face would be forever remembered, his pallid complexion, pursed lips and narrow moustache looming enigmatically out of a dark background, atop evening dress, adorned with the sensual splash of a white orchid in his buttonhole. This painting, now in the Musée d'Orsay, captures Proust eternally as a twenty-one-year-old socialite, ironically perhaps for one whose novel shows him to be so exceptionally alert to the mutability of the human body and the effects of the passing of time.

In 1891, as Blanche worked on his portrait, Oscar Wilde published *The Picture of Dorian Gray* and visited Paris. One might anticipate that a meeting between the notorious Wilde and the impressionable young Proust would have been a momentous occasion. It is not certain, however, that they actually met.[2] Two years later Proust's first sustained creative piece, 'Violante ou la mondanité' [Violante, or Worldly Vanities], was published in *Le Banquet.* Thereafter short stories, criticism, satirical sketches and essays were published in *La Revue blanche* (a prestigious journal which provided a platform for writers such as Verlaine, Mallarmé and Gide) as well as other journals and papers. In the salons of Mme Straus, Mme de Caillavet and Madeleine Lemaire he met major artistic figures of all stripes: the actress Sarah Bernhardt, poets such as José-Maria de Heredia and Leconte de Lisle, painters including Degas and Puvis de Chavannes (Lemaire herself was a painter); as well as aristocrats and royals including Charles Haas and the Princesse Mathilde. Proust, whose background was solidly *haut bourgeois*, gained access to these social arenas where titled nobility rubbed shoulders with the artistic elite by dint of his ability to charm and entertain with his conversation, wit and considerable intellect. His interactions with the prominent worldly figures of his day exposed him to intrigues, to quirks of language, conventions of behaviour, patterns of prejudice and pretension – in short, gave him a sort of sociological training. The salons were the preserve of the wealthy, but they displayed to Proust's sensibilities deeper laws and configurations of human interaction that could be found throughout the social spectrum, as his lengthy conversations with domestics and hotel and delivery staff would later confirm.

In Madeleine Lemaire's salon Proust became acquainted with the dandy and poet count Robert de Montesquiou (1855–1921), one of the period's most remarkable figures. A decadent aesthete with wealth, pomposity and idiosyncrasy in vast measure, aspects of his behaviour and eccentricities fed into Proust's fictional baron de Charlus. The decadent novelist J. K. Huysmans had already drawn heavily on Montesquiou as a model for Jean Des Esseintes, the protagonist in his 1884 novel *A rebours* [*Against Nature*], which is thought to have influenced Wilde's *Dorian Gray*. Besides Montesquiou, *chez* Lemaire Proust also met a brilliant young composer named Reynaldo Hahn. His infatuation with Hahn lasted approximately two years but their friendship endured Proust's lifetime. His early letters to Hahn, frequently signed 'Your pony', reveal how rapidly his amorous devotions developed. In the Parisian salons as well as in country residences (such as Lemaire's château de Réveillon at which Proust and Hahn spent a month in 1894), musical recitals were heard, plays and paintings discussed and the polemics – and gossip – of the day were debated. A subject that began in 1894 to pique the interest of chattering socialites, bourgeoisie and working class alike was the case of Alfred Dreyfus.

A Jewish captain on the General Staff, Dreyfus was accused of having passed information to the Germans, convicted of treason and sent, for life, to the penal colony on Devil's Island off the coast of French Guiana. In 1896, suspecting that Dreyfus was being framed to protect a non-Jewish officer, Colonel Picquart proved that the evidence against Dreyfus – a memorandum stolen from the German embassy in Paris – had been written by another man, Major Esterhazy. The latter, however, was acquitted and Picquart jailed. This turn of events led to a public outcry and demands for a retrial of Dreyfus. Emile Zola (1840–1902), in a series of articles in the *Figaro* newspaper, called for truth and justice, protesting vociferously against the military cover-up and the systemic anti-Semitism of the time. Proust and other *Dreyfusards* campaigned amongst writers and public figures for signatures on a petition backing Zola's critique of the military's juridical violations. Proust famously won Anatole France's influential signature for the cause. The drama reached its peak with the publication in January 1898 of Zola's open letter 'J'accuse' and, the following day, the petition against the authorities, the 'Manifesto of the Intellectuals'. Tried for defamation, Zola was sentenced to a year in prison but fled to England, avoiding this fate. Dreyfus was retried but found guilty again in 1899; it was not until 1906 that he was rehabilitated.

Proust is often represented as an ivory-tower aesthete but his commitment and action during the Dreyfus Affair cast him in a different light; indeed, the ways in which intellectuals were galvanized in public support of the cause anticipated the conception of socio-political engagement that characterized much French thinking and writing in the early and mid twentieth century. The Affair coloured the political landscape in France for over a decade; the tensions and tribulations it brought to all levels of French society are reflected in Proust's novel.

Proust achieved his '*licence*' degree in Philosophy in 1895 and in June 1896 a collection of his writings, *Les Plaisirs et les jours* [*Pleasures and Days*], was published in a luxury edition illustrated by Madeleine Lemaire. The book did little to change Proust's public image as a dilettante, a social climber and a snob. The following month, however, his article 'Contre l'obscurité' [Against Obscurity] was published. In it he takes issue directly with the aesthetics of symbolists such as Mallarmé. Proust begins to set out his own artistic agenda, writing forcefully in reaction to an influential current of the time: the article offers a glimpse of the writer, hitherto sheltered under the carapace of the socialite, who has thought deeply on the role of art and the function of the artist in his age.

From June 1895 Proust had a post working in the Mazarine library; or he would have done had his evasions (citing health problems) and nepotistic string-pulling not permitted him to take repeated leaves of absence. His leave was made permanent in 1900. During these years Proust spent time in Dieppe, Belle-Île and Beg Meil in Brittany, in Kreuznach in Germany with his mother, and in Fontainebleau. The sketches and notes for a novelistic project, never finished, posthumously known as *Jean Santeuil*, were drafted during this time. From his letters we know that Proust was also working his way through a substantial collection of European writers: Rousseau's *Confessions*, Balzac and Sainte-Beuve in large doses, Shakespeare, Goethe and George Eliot. His reading at Fontainebleau in October 1896 alone (*Julius Caesar*, *Anthony and Cleopatra*, *Wilhelm Meister*, *Middlemarch*) represents a remarkable sweep of tales of love, ambition, deception and self-exploration, all concerns that take their place in Proust's later writings.

The second half of the 1890s witnessed a waning in Proust and Hahn's closeness; Proust's affections were growing for Lucien Daudet, younger son of renowned writer Alphonse Daudet (1840–97). In February 1897 Jean Lorrain, a novelist and journalist whose voluble homophobia was as notorious as his closeted homosexuality, published an article mocking *Pleasures and Days* and casting aspersions about the nature of Proust and Daudet's relationship. At the time, a public insinuation of homosexuality, however accurate it may have been, was perceived as an affront to the integrity of the accused and to the honour of his family name. The oddity of this situation – a known homosexual publicly deriding another – is characteristic of the attitudes of the period to same-sex relations. What Lorrain reviled (and what he perceived between Proust and Daudet) was homosexuality taking the form of effeminacy, un-manly behaviour. Strictures of form in society dictated that same-sex preference and practices should be expressed and satisfied discreetly and in private: the acceptable face of masculinity was a virile one and so Proust, fearful of the impact Lorrain's affront might have on his parents, challenged him to a duel with pistols. Shots were fired on 6 February, neither man was injured and the matter was deemed resolved.

Some time in 1897 Proust discovered the work of the English art historian and critic John Ruskin (1819–1900). For several years Proust absorbed himself in Ruskin's *œuvre*, collaborating closely with his mother and Hahn's English cousin Marie Nordlinger to translate two of Ruskin's well-known works, *The Bible of Amiens* (1885) and *Sesame and Lilies* (1865): the translations were published, respectively, in 1904 and 1906. In 1900 Proust visited several of the French cathedrals Ruskin had studied, as well as Venice and Padua. In 1901, after these trips and the concerted focus of his work, Proust's health was poor, but he managed, the following year, to make visits and to attend several exhibitions across Belgium and the Netherlands. This activity was pleasing to Proust's parents who had feared he might never combine well-being with the volition necessary to commit to any task of real substance.

Proust's mother had an operation in the summer of 1898 to remove a cancerous tumour; she regained sufficient strength to travel with her son to Venice and Padua in 1900 but was no longer her resilient self. In November 1903 her husband, by now commander in the Legion of Honour for his distinctions in medical science, died suddenly. In September 1905, still distraught at her loss, after repeated attacks of uraemia, the complaint from which her mother had suffered, Jeanne Proust died of acute kidney failure. 'She takes my life with her', wrote Proust in a letter at the time, 'like Papa had taken hers.'[3] The solidity and comfort of the family unit was shattered and Proust, fragile of health, was alone in the world with his grief.

The two brothers shared the considerable family fortune. Although this included a substantial monthly income Proust was incorrigibly extravagant and lived constantly in fear of becoming insolvent. Towards the end of his year of mourning, he resolved to move to new surroundings, something he had always found debilitatingly difficult. He moved to his uncle's old apartment at 102 boulevard Haussmann, a property his mother had known well, which pleased him. Such consolation notwithstanding, the move was an enormous upheaval: the noise of traffic and passers-by outside and renovation work within the building troubled him; he feared the levels of dust, and pollen from the trees. In August 1907 he went to Cabourg, a destination again determined by fond memories of time spent there with his mother, and this trip – the first of a succession of summers spent in the seaside resort – marked a number of new beginnings.

There he met Alfred Agostinelli, a nineteen-year-old driver, in whose taxi he visited many nearby sights of interest and in whom he found an employee, companion and, ultimately, an object of love. Agostinelli served as Proust's driver in 1907 and 1908 before disappearing from view until 1913 when he contacted Proust looking for work. Proust already had a driver in Paris, Odilon Albaret (whose wife Céleste, from 1914 until Proust's death, served as his housekeeper), but he nevertheless agreed to take on Agostinelli as a secretary and lodged him and his partner Anna in the apartment on boulevard Haussmann. Proust preferred to keep this arrangement quiet; tensions grew between them (primarily because of Proust's jealousy) and yet still he spent great sums of money on the younger man. Agostinelli, however, fled without warning to the south coast of France in December 1913. Proust did his best but failed to make him return. The following summer, having enrolled himself in a flying school near Antibes under the name 'Marcel Swann', on just his second solo flight, against his instructor's advice Agostinelli attempted a low turn, crashed into the sea and drowned with his sinking aircraft. For Proust, an 'integral part of [his] existence' had been stolen from him by the fierce, sudden finality of death.[4]

Many aspects of Proust and Agostinelli's relationship work their way into the *Search*, above all in the later, tortuous unfoldings of the Narrator's relation with Albertine, written after Agostinelli's death. For Proust the period between meeting Agostinelli in Cabourg in August 1907 and his death in 1914 was one of unprecedented, intense creative activity.

Near the start of 1908 Proust began making notes and jottings for a novel in a notebook, the *Carnet de 1908*, which has entries dating up to 1912 and is a vital document in understanding the genesis and evolution of the various scenes and ideas that would eventually combine to form *In Search of Lost Time*. As Proust's creative cogs began to turn, in January 1908 there broke an intriguing news scandal: an engineer named Lemoine convinced the president of De Beers that he could *make* diamonds and successfully swindled a sizeable sum of money from him. Proust wrote accounts of the improbable affair in the style of several major writers, which were published to great acclaim. Between late 1908 and August 1909 he also filled ten school notebooks with material we now know as *Contre Sainte-Beuve* [*Against Sainte-Beuve*].

Sleeping (or trying to sleep) during the day and working all night, buoyed up against asthma and fatigue by medicines and stimulants had long been Proust's *modus vivendi* and it was how he set about constructing his novel. By 1909 he had a fragmentary draft, although its boundaries were decidedly indeterminate. The cork lining, insulation from the ills of the outside world, went up in boulevard Haussmann whilst Proust was in Cabourg in July 1910. The following summer he wrote that his novel was 'an extremely considerable work, at least in terms of its mad length' and that in order to finish it, he should like the assistance of a secretary 'for two or three months'.[5] Eleven years later Proust would die before his final revisions to this most 'considerable work' were complete.

In October 1912 the overall working title was *Les Intermittences du cœur* [*The Intermittencies of the Heart*] and the work was to consist of two volumes, *Le Temps perdu* and *Le Temps retrouvé*. After refusals from a number of publishers, including the *Nouvelle Revue Française* (NRF), whose decision fell to André Gide, who may not have bothered to read the manuscript, Proust finally decided to publish at his own expense. Terms were agreed with Grasset in March 1913, and Proust soon set about revising the proofs. Finally, in November 1913 *Swann's Way* was published, announced as the first of three volumes of *A la recherche du temps perdu*, the second and third advertised as *Le Côté de Guermantes* and *Le Temps retrouvé*.

The novel never ceased to swell between its inception and the publication of the first volume; so it continued to grow organically for nine more years until Proust's death in 1922 and beyond to September 1927 when the publication of *Time Regained*, by then the seventh volume of the *Search*, closed the loop of this *sui generis* publishing adventure. *Swann's Way* received mixed reviews, but soon some of those who had earlier knocked Proust's project, or had prejudged it because of his reputation, were avowing their admiration, among them Gide, who went some way towards atoning for his prior lapse by suggesting that the NRF publish the rest of the *Search*. The contract was finalized in 1916 and the publication of the novel was resumed, between *NRF* covers, in 1919.

It was just a month after the publication of *Swann* that Agostinelli disappeared from Proust's apartment. This traumatic chapter in Proust's personal life diluted the joy that publication should have brought. Agostinelli's death the following summer struck another body-blow to Proust's already weak frame. *The Guermantes Way*, the second volume announced at the time of the publication of *Swann*, should have been published in 1915 but Bernard Grasset was mobilized and his publishing house closed down (Proust's ill health kept him out of active service, although the fear of medical checks and the possibility of enlistment kept him constantly on edge). As a result this volume also swelled in 1914–15, cleaving into what we now know as *A l'ombre des jeunes filles en fleurs* [*Within a Budding Grove*] and *The Guermantes Way*.

As Proust's novel hypertrophied from half a million words before the war to around one-and-a-quarter million words after it, violent conflict was destroying human life on an unprecedented scale. Proust followed the developments of the war in their minutest details, reading seven newspapers a day. He was critical of what he viewed as expressions of jingoistic nationalism from many writers of the time such as Montesquiou and Léon Daudet, elder brother of Lucien. His health was poor, the hours he kept were unconventional, but he continued to write huge numbers of letters and to go out periodically in search of details he would stitch into the fabric of his novel. He attended concerts and theatrical performances, including those of the 'Ballets russes', brought to Paris by Sergei Diaghilev. In addition to the sociological and intellectual inquisitiveness that could be sated in the boxes of the Opéra or in the dining rooms of the Ritz, at Albert le Cuziat's male brothel Proust was also able to satisfy his libidinal curiosities. Le Cuziat's establishment was a source of gossip, gratification and insights (sometimes voyeuristic ones) into the normally concealed workings of desire. From individuals like le Cuziat, the wide range of men who used his brothel and, as of 1917, Olivier Dabascat, the *maître d'hôtel* at the Ritz, Proust availed himself of a multiplicity of perspectives on the world that add a persuasive sense of depth and texture to the social landscapes of his novel.

In 1918, Proust was in the streets during a German bombing raid on Paris. Later that year he received further intimations of his mortality when he was struck briefly by facial paralysis and light aphasia (short spells of being unable to recognize language). The following year brought laryngitis but also long-awaited recognition in the form of the Goncourt Prize for *Within a Budding Grove*, published in June along with the *NRF* printing of *Swann* and a volume of collected shorter writings, *Pastiches et mélanges*. The new laureate, however, was struggling with the mundanity of moving house again. The building in boulevard Haussmann was sold to a bank and Proust had to move out. In October 1919 he moved to what would be his final residence at 44 rue Hamelin.

Proust's ailments and his long-term enthusiasm for self-administering large quantities of barbiturates, caffeine and other substances had taken their toll on his body. His deteriorating eyesight and respiratory troubles slowed down his corrections to *The Guermantes Way* and although the award, in September 1920, of the Legion of Honour lifted his spirits he still worried about whether people would actually read his work. *The Guermantes Way* and the first part of *Sodom and Gomorrah* appeared between October 1920 and May 1921. The following month, feeble and pale from medication and insomnia, Proust ventured out to an exhibition of Dutch Masters where he saw Vermeer's *View of Delft*, a painting he had last seen in the Hague in 1902. Some time between 1916 and 1922, he wrote the word '*Fin*' [The End] at the foot of the page that brings the novel to its close. When this word was written, his single unstinting task was complete. 'I'm no longer anxious', he told Céleste Albaret, 'my work can appear. I won't have given my life for nothing.'[6]

The second part of *Sodom and Gomorrah* appeared in May 1922, and from about this time Proust's diet consisted largely of ice cream and iced beer: it was all he could palate after having burnt his digestive tract taking insufficiently diluted dry adrenaline. Eventually he developed bronchitis, which in turn became pneumonia. On 18 November Proust died with his housekeeper and his brother at his side. The latter and Gaston Gallimard edited and published the novel's remaining volumes, *La Prisonnière* [*The Captive*] (1923), *Albertine disparue* [*The Fugitive*] (1925) and *Time Regained* (1927).

The smooth-cheeked artist of Blanche's painting was no more; on his deathbed Proust's face was heavily bearded, the searching eyes now closed and darkly ringed. Existence for the artist was over, his form etched by Paul Helleu and photographed by Man Ray for posterity, their respective media pointing symbolically backwards and forwards to the old and new centuries to which Proust belonged. As for his work – the monstrous work that had taken so long to materialize, that tortured him, drained him of his vitality yet equally gave him purpose and fulfilment – life was just beginning.

Contexts

In *Time Regained*, after long illness and absence from society life, the Narrator returns to one last matinée at which he meets many figures from his distant past. Time has changed them, aged and distorted their faces, their gait. M. d'Argencourt in particular catches the Narrator's eye:

> [It was] as a puppet, a trembling puppet with a beard of white wool, that I saw him being shakily put through his paces …, in a puppet-show which was both scientific and philosophical and in which he served – as though it had been at the same time a funeral oration and a lecture at the Sorbonne – both as a text for a sermon on the vanity of all things and as an object lesson in natural history. (*TR*, 290; 2306)

No longer in control of its movements, the human body is depicted as puppet-like. The spectacle is described as scientific and philosophical, then the analogies used expand its potential interpretation yet further: a funeral oration might have a spiritual or philosophical dimension but is unlikely to be scientific; a university lecture might be scientific or philosophical. The further suggestions of a sermon on *vanitas* and a lesson in natural history again reinforce the original terms whilst expanding their range further still. In offering readers these divergent yet complementary possible contexts for thinking about this *guignol*-like figure, Proust underlines the multiple ways in which people and events may be viewed and understood. The Narrator continues:

> A puppet-show, yes, but one in which, in order to identify the puppets with the people whom one had known in the past, it was necessary to read on several planes at once, planes that lay behind the visible aspect of the puppets and gave them depth and forced one … to make a strenuous intellectual effort; one was obliged to study them at the same time with one's eyes and with one's memory. (*TR*, 290, trans. mod.; 2307)

'To identify', 'to read', 'to study': the verbs used here remind us how Proust's novel is concerned throughout its duration with the pursuit of knowledge. The *Search* repeatedly asks us to make a strenuous intellectual effort of the sort the Narrator feels himself drawn into here, and the method he identifies – that is, attempting to read on different levels at once – offers us a useful analogy for thinking about Proust's novel in its cultural and intellectual contexts. Any single page (indeed, any single sentence) of the *Search* bears inlaid in its imagery, its grand sweeps and its sub-clauses references and allusions to events within the novel, and those of the period in which it is set, to people and to works of art real and imaginary. If we want to get the most from our reading, to revel in the sort of pluralities exposed in the passages quoted above, we have to seek to emulate the Narrator's efforts at interpretive simultaneity. The present chapter aims to assist readers in so doing by offering a number of contextual frameworks for Proust's novel.[1]

I will consider three broad domains: politics and society; science, technology and medicine; literature, philosophy and the arts. These divisions, as will soon become apparent, are relatively arbitrary given the interwoven nature of the events of the period, but reading these sections will give a sense of the heady array of developments and discoveries that drove France ever further into the realm of modernity between the time of the Paris Commune and the aftermath of the First World War. These are contexts in which we might situate Proust's novel, a project whose vast ambition aligns it with the dynamic, forward-reaching period in which it was produced, yet which equally far exceeds that period, making such demands as it does on the time, intellect and memory of its readers as directly to contravene that same era's imperative for speed in all things. This very strangeness of Proust's novel (a strangeness, as Harold Bloom has noted, that often characterizes canonical works) places it somehow beyond the reasonable expectations of *any* present moment yet gives it a bewildering appeal to readers far removed in time and space from the rarefied atmospheres of post-Commune and pre-war Paris.

Politics and society

Proust's life and his work straddle three major eras in French history: the aftermath of the Paris Commune; the years of the Third French Republic known as the *belle époque*; and the period of the First World War and its immediate aftermath. He was born shortly after the time of the Commune, when the working classes assumed control of government in the French capital following extended civic unrest after defeat in the Franco-Prussian war (July 1870 to

January 1871). While the city his parents fled, fearing for their lives, was one so wracked by conflict that its inhabitants were reduced to killing and eating garden birds and animals from the zoo in order to survive, the bulk of Proust's active, creative years were those of the *belle époque*, the time from around the beginning of the Dreyfus Affair to the outbreak of the First World War. For the affluent, amongst whom Proust moved in his adolescence and his adult life, this was a world of banquets, champagne and finery; but it was a world which, in June 1914, was precipitated into the largest, most bloody conflict the world had ever witnessed.[2]

The July Monarchy of 1830 ended in 1848 when Louis-Philippe d'Orléans abdicated. The Second Republic was proclaimed and Louis-Napoleon Bonaparte, whose uncle had been defeated at Waterloo in 1814, was elected President. After a *coup d'état* against the constitution in 1851, he proclaimed himself Emperor Napoleon III the following year and by the mid 1850s Baron Haussmann, Napoleon's prefect of the Seine, was well under way with his project of reconstruction and renewal, pulling down much of the insalubrious, old Paris and building a city fit to call itself an Imperial Capital. Napoleon's disastrous war with Prussia, however, ending in French defeat and his capture at Sedan, near the Belgian border, in September 1870, marked the beginning of the end of the Second Empire. The Third French Republic was proclaimed on 4 September 1871 when Proust was not yet two months old.

These and subsequent events (above all the Dreyfus Affair and the First World War) do feature in Proust's novel but not because he seeks to offer a chronicle of the Third Republic. Rather, they feature in the conversation and debates of the characters and as forces that shape and alter these individuals through time. As Malcolm Bowie puts it, 'political parties and factions are named but not described. Upheavals within the Church, the army or the judiciary are notable only for the shock waves and the ripples of curiosity they send through dinners and receptions'.[3] This is not to say that Proust was uninterested in politics and current affairs; he was an engaged reader of newspapers and incorrigibly inquisitive, but what interested him above all were the behavioural motivations of the individual in his or her relationships, not the unfolding of major events per se. These were only interesting for Proust when they permitted him insight into the functioning of the psyche, the workings of the desirous mind or the dynamics of individuals' behaviour when they 'belong' to a certain social group. It is arguably Proust's (and his Narrator's) lack of belonging to a single definable group that permits the depth of analysis that he offers. As one of his biographers puts it, Proust 'possessed both a grasp of how society works and a sufficient distance from it to view it objectively and then to write about it'.[4]

The society of the Third Republic was many-layered, deeply divided along class lines, formed of many discrete sets: some were dwindling remnants of times past (such as the old nobility, centred in Paris in the faubourg Saint-Germain), others were gradually swelling in size, confidence and clout, namely the various strata of the wealthy – and ambitious – bourgeoisie. Balzac's *Comédie Humaine* had chronicled the rise of money and ambition through the societal landscapes of the First Empire and the Restoration; Proust's novel goes on to explore a variety of social milieux of the *belle époque* and we can trace the trajectories of various individuals (such as Bloch, Odette, Mme Verdurin) who successfully move between different social stations.

Robert de Saint-Loup-en-Bray, whose uncles are the Duc de Guermantes and the Baron de Charlus, and whose father, the Comte de Marsantes, was killed in the Franco-Prussian War, is a pivotal figure in the *Search*'s social drama as a character who challenges conventions. His interest in socialism and in the philosophy of Friedrich Nietzsche (1844–1900) reflects prominent currents of thought of the period but is quite at odds with his privileged upbringing and social status. When the Duc de Guermantes hears of his nephew's *dreyfusard* sympathies, his concern is redoubled by the thought that this radical point of view will lead to Saint-Loup being blackballed for election to the Jockey Club, *belle époque* Paris's most exclusive gentlemen's club. The Duc's response is revealing: 'I do claim to move with the times; but damn it all, when one goes by the name of Marquis de Saint-Loup one isn't a Dreyfusard' (*G*, 268; 926). Proust here underlines the absurdity of the partisanal divisions by which French society was riven during the Dreyfus Affair.

Given the prolonged nature of the Affair it was common for individuals to change sides as events unfolded. Proclaiming one's allegiance to one or other camp was a means of gaining access to certain salons or social circles that would otherwise remain closed. Such turns of the social kaleidoscope (this is a preferred image of Proust's for the realignments and reconfigurations of the people and places of the social world) are traced in the *Search*, scrutinized for what they reveal about the laws – and the vicissitudes – of human behaviour.

The Narrator's grandfather's treatment of Bloch in 'Combray' (*SW*, 107–8; 80–1) illustrates the anti-Semitism that was not uncommon in French society before the time of the Affair and was fomented by anti-*dreyfusard* agitators as it developed. Édouard Drumont had published the best-selling anti-Semitic tract *La France juive* [*Jewish France*] in 1886, which blamed the country's ills on the Jews; he formed the French Anti-Semitic League in 1889, which had its own newspaper *La Libre Parole*. Religious and racial tensions, however, were not the only ones that rendered unsteady the social edifice of the Third Republic. Perhaps more complex were the rifts between the different social castes.

Saint-Loup in his military role is used by Proust further to illustrate the manifold social morphology of the period. The Narrator's friend descends from a line of ancient nobility traceable back centuries. As a non-commissioned officer Saint-Loup answers to Captain – the Prince – de Borodino. One might fairly expect these men, a marquis and a prince, to share some common ground. Proust, however, lays bare the fine distinctions between Saint-Loup's *ancien régime* nobility and Borodino's more recent Napoleonic title. Saint-Loup's attitude towards the lower classes is one of 'patronising affability': he is casually cordial with them, condescendingly believing that this might flatter them. The individuals Saint-Loup treats in this way, by contrast, are addressed by Borodino 'with a majestic affability, in which a reserve full of grandeur tempered the smiling good-fellowship that came naturally to him, in a tone marked at once by a genuine kindliness and a stiffness deliberately assumed' (*G*, 144, trans. mod.; 845–6). Borodino prefers the company of common men, knowing that the middle class 'was the great reservoir from which the first Emperor had chosen his marshals and his nobles' (*G*, 144–5; 846), yet he keeps them at a greater distance than does Saint-Loup, on whom Borodino looks down 'from the height of his Imperial grandeur' (*G*, 143; 845), taking the scion of old nobility for an inferior who merely *thinks* himself superior. Snobbishness is found at all levels of society and, as Proust shows, it can take many unexpected forms.

The *Search*, however, is far from exclusively devoted to high society. Balbec, the thriving (fictional) seaside resort of which so many in reality blossomed on the Normandy coast at the end of the nineteenth century, offers a fish-bowl-like social arena for all the classes to intermingle; here the upper crust, extricated from their sealed Parisian salons, become visible to the lower classes. As the *belle époque* saw the decline of the old aristocracy it also witnessed, in parallel with expanding commerce and industry, the steady rise of the bourgeoisie. Mme Verdurin, for example, 'came from a respectable middle-class family, excessively rich and wholly undistinguished' (*SW*, 225; 157). Her salon welcomes all stripes, from the lower middle classes to the professionals of the *grande bourgeoisie* – actresses, artists, doctors, academics – anyone who is not 'a bore'. The criss-crossing trajectories of the Verdurins and their 'faithful', Cottard, Brichot, Elstir, Odette and others, can be tracked from the little clan in 'Swann in Love' through to the apotheosis of Mme Verdurin (after twice being widowed and twice remarrying) as the Princesse de Guermantes in *Time Regained*. Their loves, triumphs, betrayals and disappointments, by turns comic and revelatory of human frailties, form an instructive social pageant yet one to whose fragility, to whose potential to crumble with the next turn of the kaleidoscope, Proust keeps us always alert.

Science, technology and medicine

If received opinions are to be believed, *In Search of Lost Time* is not the sort of book in which one would find much space given over to the cold calculations and hard edges of science and technology. Proust's, the argument goes, is a book about sensation and memory, about liquescent crumbs of cake and wistful reminiscence, page after metaphor-laden page of lengthy sentences and prim aestheticism; this is not a book in which one would find telephone exchanges and telegrams, bicycles, central heating, elevators and aeroplanes. Or is it? The answer, of course, is that it is.

Shortly before Proust's eighteenth birthday the Eiffel Tower was opened, the entrance arch for the 1889 *Exposition Universelle* marking the centenary of the Revolution. The Paris *Exposition* of 1867 had attracted some eleven million visitors and the centennial show was even bigger, drawing over twenty-five million throughout its six-month duration. France – and Paris in particular – considered itself the heart of a brave new industrial world, a booming world of mass consumption. The 1880s and 1890s saw considerable technological leaps forward, many of which find their way into Proust's novel. The telephone, invented in 1876, spread in its use and accessibility during this time and Proust makes us look on what is now a mundane feature of our everyday existence with new eyes: the Narrator ponders at length this marvel that obliterates distance, uniting disparate places and people in a magical, disembodied encounter (*G*, 146–52; 847–51). The coming of indoor electrical lighting marks another step in Mme Verdurin's rise (see *BG*, 211; *JF*, 481). The 1890s saw increased comfort and practicality in bicycle design and with this came not just increased speed of travel but also liberation from now impractical and antiquated conventions of dress, particularly for women. As bicycles became more affordable, they permitted a certain dissolution of class boundaries: the highways and byways of, for instance, the Normandy coast offered rather more opportunities for the intermixing of the classes than the rigid structures of society had hitherto permitted.

Perhaps disappointingly for those whose conception of Proust is limited to the romanticized, blissful moments of recall provoked by lime-blossom tea and cake, the developments of modern technology also have important roles to play in the unfolding of the themes of time, space, memory and identity. Motorcars, as well as *madeleines*, teach the Narrator valuable lessons. The number of automobiles on French roads grew dramatically from the turn of the century: there were approximately 3,000 in 1900 and by 1913, the year *Swann's Way* was published, this number had risen to around 100,000. Motorcars, like the railways that had come before them, have a powerful effect on our perception of time and space, serving to link – like the telephone – what had previously been thought to be irrevocably separate. Proust was an inquisitive passenger in Agostinelli's taxi in 1907 and these early trips provided materials for an article, 'Impressions de route en automobile' [Impressions of Riding in an Automobile], published in *Le Figaro* that year. The conjunction of past and present, as so often in Proust, is beautifully encapsulated in this article in the image of Agostinelli using the lamps from his car to illuminate the façade of Lisieux cathedral at night, 'casting up to the sculptures the greeting of the present whose light now did no more than serve better to read the lessons of the past'.[5] In the *Search* the Narrator reflects on the different intensities of sensation afforded the traveller by rail and road transit (the latter allowing us to follow 'more closely, in a more intimate congruity, the various gradations by which the surface of the earth is diversified'; *BG*, 255; *JF*, 512). Lying in his bed in Paris, in *The Captive*, the heady smell of petrol fumes from a car in the street below provokes for the Narrator an involuntary recollection of excursions near Balbec during happier days (*C*, 469–70; *P*, 1912).

Proust perhaps unexpectedly, then, finds a place in his grand aesthetic project for the technological innovations of his time – the motorcar, bicycle and telephone (as well as telegrams, the player piano and the elevator). The events of the novel, however, play themselves out during a period not just of technological advancement but also of major developments in science and medicine. In philosophy and psychology (and the developing field of psychoanalysis) debates developed about our conceptions of 'private' or subjectively experienced time, whilst in the domains of physics and mathematics the very nature of time and space was being challenged and rethought.[6]

With his Special Theory of Relativity of 1905 and the General Theory of 1916, Albert Einstein revolutionized the way time, space, movement and gravity are understood.[7] In *Within a Budding Grove* the Narrator considers at length how it was for him to observe the constant motion of the young girls' accelerated bodies along the strand at Balbec, in contradistinction to the other visitors on the beach and the promenade. Repeatedly in the novel he alludes to the different gearings of time, the apparent accelerations and diminutions of the pace at which we experience time's passing; and at the close of the first chapter of *The Fugitive* the Narrator makes the following remarks, in which we can recognize how scientific developments are recruited analogically by Proust, in this case to illustrate the rigours of dealing with loss: 'as there is a geometry in space, so there is a psychology in time, in which the calculations of a plane psychology would no longer be accurate because we should not be taking account of Time and one of the forms that it assumes, forgetting' (*F*, 637; *AD*, 2023). In losing Albertine the Narrator gains a new sensitivity to time and forgetting, forces which bring an additional dimension to our emotional universe. A number of critics in the 1920s drew parallels between the impact of Proust's and Einstein's work in their respective fields and although Proust was flattered by the suggestion he was reluctant to endorse it for fear that readers might interpret the link as one of comparable abstraction and incomprehensibility, rather than something more positive. He did concede in a letter, however, that 'We [Proust and Einstein] have, it seems, an analogous way of deforming Time'.[8]

In composing the metaphors that add layer upon layer of referential richness to his novel, Proust drew widely on biology and botany, entomology, chemistry, physics and physiology. His father's profession had exposed him from an early age to the language and literature of medicine and these play a prominent role in the novel on at least two levels. First, the Narrator suffers from fragile health and is personally concerned by and well informed about medical matters. Second, his interest in medicine is disseminated throughout the text at the level of metaphor, as infections, suffering, disease, medication, palliative care and the like are enlisted by the Narrator as he seeks through language to get ever closer to an accurate approximation of human experience, be it of love, loss, jealousy or passion. 'Swann in Love' is an extended account of love as malady and its effects on a patient whose gradually degenerating bill of health foreshadows many of the symptoms and the prognosis of the Narrator in his subsequent relation with Albertine.

Proust's father was at the forefront of medical science and his works, such as *L'Hygiène du neurasthénique* [*How to Live with Neurasthenia*], co-authored with Gilbert Ballet in 1897, broke new ground in the understanding of nervous illness of precisely the sort from which his son suffered. Neurasthenia, or nervous exhaustion, whose symptoms could include fatigue, headaches, insomnia and neuralgia was a medical condition identified by the American neurologist George Beard in the 1860s and made widely known in his work of 1881, *American Nervousness: Its Causes and Consequences*. The increased speeds and intensities of modern life, argued Beard, had led to the spread of nervous disorders. Proust *père* and others continued Beard's work, seeking to understand the blight of nervous illness in a European context. Asthma (again a condition from which Professor Proust's son suffered) was thought to be one such illness. The interconnections between the mind, the nervous system, the emotions and the body were explored in the 1880s and 1890s in the medical sciences, experimental psychology, sexology and philosophy – all branches of enquiry seeking recognizable principles and systematized knowledge – and this diversity of approaches to the understanding of the functioning and frailties of the human form translates directly into the pages of the *Search*, which even in its title mirrors the questing, knowledge-seeking flavour of its age.

While love is often metaphorically medicalized in Proust's novel, in the same period sexual behaviour was a central topic, often related to mental health, in the discourses of medical science. Certain sexual practices were believed to lead to mental problems and certain mental illnesses and 'aberrant' behaviours were thought to be hereditary. Medical-neurological theories of degeneracy as well as Hippolyte Taine's historical conception of the importance of '*race, milieu et moment*' in the development of the individual find their greatest literary exploration in the twenty volumes of Émile Zola's novelistic history of the Rougon-Macquart family (published 1871–93); they also find later echoes in Proust's novel. Homosexuality was medicalized, deemed to be an illness, or a vice that should be treated like an ailment. Masturbation was, as William Carter has summarized, 'condemned by parents, priests, teachers and doctors';[9] when Proust's parents learnt of their adolescent son's compulsive masturbation and his advances towards his male friends, Professor Proust felt it appropriate to send him to a brothel as a 'solution'.[10]

It is against this backcloth of attitudes to sexuality that Proust, who had already fought a duel over insinuations of homosexuality, set about writing his novel in which a broad array of sexual preferences is explored and discussed. His radically modern conception that each individual's sexuality was a shifting conglomerate of traits both masculine and feminine, with desire leading each of us to focus on different objects, male or female, depending on our particular disposition at a given moment, anticipates the findings of Alfred Kinsey's research into human sexuality in the 1940s and 1950s. Although Proust frequently refers to homosexuality in terms redolent of the dominant, conventional mindset of his time (in *Sodom and Gomorrah* homosexuals are described as 'a race upon which a curse is laid'; *SG*, 17; 1219), he also does much, as Malcolm Bowie puts it, 'imaginatively [to reinvent] the straightforwardness of non-straight sex'.[11]

Literature, philosophy and the arts

To seek to survey the artistic and intellectual contexts of Proust's life and work in any more than a summary form is a task well beyond the scope of this book. Proust's *Search* is a remarkable repository of reference and allusion not just to the works produced or popular in its own time but also to several centuries of philosophy, literature, visual art and music. Swann, for example, procrastinates over an unfinished study of Vermeer (1632–75); Charlus instructs Morel on his interpretation of Beethoven's (1770–1827) late quartets; and the Narrator gives Albertine an impromptu tutorial on novelistic technique in Thomas Hardy (1840–1928), Dostoevsky (1821–81) and Stendhal (1783–1842).

To think, then, of the intellectual and artistic contexts of Proust's life and work we need to do so on 'several planes at once': we need to look back towards the nineteenth century and well beyond (Proust is frequently close in style to the seventeenth-century *moralistes* La Bruyère and La Rochefoucauld and shares traits with the memoirist Saint-Simon). We should also look to the *belle époque*, the war and post-war periods in order to gauge how Proust can be understood in the context of contemporary trends, including the shifting literary currents of Symbolism, Decadence and Naturalism, evolutions in visual art from Impressionism through Pointillism, Fauvism and Cubism, as well as wider intellectual movements such as Futurism and Dada. It is also possible to consider Proust as a central figure of European Modernism: his work can be profitably understood in the context of a canon of early-twentieth-century writers, including Mann, Kafka, Woolf and Joyce, all of whom contributed to shifting radically the scope and potential of literary creativity.

The products of the creative imagination and the intellect were Proust's oxygen from very early in his life: in practically every letter he wrote he relates details of his reading, reflects on recent theatrical performances or seeks details of exhibitions or recitals. Some 8,000 publications and works of art are mentioned in his correspondence; the index of literary and artistic works mentioned in the *Pléiade* edition of the *Search* runs to sixteen pages of close-packed, tiny print. But what is the function of this proliferation of references? A reader new to Proust and/or unfamiliar with the expansive and varied terrain of art, literature and thought from which he picks his points of reference can quickly become overwhelmed or dispirited. In what follows I attempt to offer a selective survey of parts of this terrain and offer some paths through it.

Growing up in the early years of the French Third Republic, Proust's education and his voluminous reading provided him with a wide-ranging knowledge of classical authors (such as Homer, Plato and Virgil) as well as French writers from the sixteenth century to his contemporaries, from Rabelais and Montaigne to Mallarmé and Henri de Régnier. In 1888, encouraging his classmate Daniel Halévy to free himself of Naturalist and Decadent tendencies in his writing, Proust suggested that he should immerse himself in a daunting diet of heavyweights, including Shakespeare, Shelley, Emerson, Goethe, Descartes, Racine and Flaubert.[12] From the two keepsake questionnaires Proust completed we gain a sense of the development of his artistic tastes during his formative years. In the second questionnaire we learn that Musset, the romantic dramatist and poet of the '*mal du siècle*' [malady of the century] has been displaced as Proust's favourite poet by Alfred de Vigny and by Baudelaire, whose collection *Les Fleurs du mal* [*The Flowers of Evil*] caused scandal and was tried for offences against public morality in 1857. Vigny was a romantic, author of 'La Maison du Berger' [The Shepherd's House] (1840–4), a long love poem Proust admired enormously and which the Narrator quotes to Albertine. The poem contains the lines:

> La distance et le temps sont vaincus. La science
> Trace autour de la terre un chemin triste et droit.
> [Distance and time are overcome. Science/Traces around the earth a
>   sad, straight path.]

In part lamenting the coming of the railways to France, these lines anticipate by over half a century Proust's own exploration, discussed above, of the impact of technological advances on our spatio-temporal perceptions. Another Vigny poem, 'The Wrath of Samson', suggested the title and provided the epigraph ('Woman shall have Gomorrah and man shall have Sodom') for *Sodom and Gomorrah*. Similarly, Baudelaire's poem 'Lesbos', banned from the original edition of *Les Fleurs du mal*, offers us insight into the veiled connotations of Proust's enigmatic title *A l'ombre des jeunes filles en fleurs*: 'Car Lesbos entre tous m'a choisi sur la terre', wrote Baudelaire, 'pour chanter le secret de ses vierges en fleurs' [For Lesbos has chosen me amongst all of earth/To sing the secret of its flowering virgins], lines quoted by Proust in his celebrated essay 'Concerning Baudelaire' of 1921.[13]

The younger Proust's preference for Musset and for the novels of George Sand (1804–76) was, most likely, inherited from his grandmother. Sand gives way in the second questionnaire to two contemporary authors, Anatole France (1844–1924) and Pierre Loti (1850–1923). Loti is referred to in *The Guermantes Way* as the sort of popular figure who would be found in the best salons, providing the hostess with valuable cultural capital; France is referred to on a number of occasions in the novel (it is suggested that he frequents Mme Verdurin's *dreyfusard* salon), and Bergotte, the *Search*'s fictional novelist, displays many of France's characteristics as a writer. This sort of melding of the real and the fictional by Proust lends depth and nuance to the *Search* as a whole. As with Loti and France, artists or works of art are often mentioned in the *Search* not for aesthetic reasons but for social ones. To talk about the right artists, to mention the right works, is to show common cause with the salon elite and thereby to be accepted. Proust also uses this attitude of considering art as a commodity to send up his pompous or vacuous characters who in reality are far removed from the possible riches art can offer. M. de Guermantes, for example, proclaims with all the assurance of a true connoisseur: 'Fra

Diavolo and the *Magic Flute,* and *Le Chalet,* and the *Marriage of Figaro,* and *Les Diamants de la couronne* – there's music for you!'; except he lays bare his ignorance by intermingling, in his role call of greats, Mozart's masterpieces with some minor comic operas of the 1830s and 1840s. 'It's the same thing in literature', he announces, ominously, 'For instance, I adore Balzac, *Le Bal de Sceaux, Les Mohicans de Paris*' (*G*, 567; 1123). The deflating truth that the second novel mentioned here is by Dumas Père and not Balzac is not acknowledged by the Narrator, but the message is clear. Art can lead us to knowledge and to beauty, it can help us understand or cope with pain; it might even offer us salvation; but for many *mondains*, art is just another social accoutrement, paraded like a flamboyant garment or a piece of jewellery, quite devoid of the potential transformative and revelatory force that the Narrator and other kindred spirits recognize it to have.

At times we find imaginary works of art being described in terms redolent of real, existing works of the period. Proust met the painter Paul Helleu (1859–1927) in Cabourg and he and the influential American James McNeill Whistler (1834–1903), whom Proust admired enormously, are important models for Elstir, the fictional painter of the *Search,* whose name echoes those of both models. The descriptions of Elstir's early mythological paintings bear striking similarities with those of Gustave Moreau (1826–98), whilst his seascapes – again, only ever existing in words on Proust's pages – put one in mind of works by Helleu and Whistler as well as Claude Monet, J.M.W. Turner and others.

To take a further example of Proust's borrowing from the major artistic currents of his time, let us consider the Narrator's earliest attempt at writing, first discussed in *Swann's Way.* His piece, a sort of prose poem, is an account of his experience of seeing the bell towers of the Martinville and Vieuxvicq churches apparently – impossibly – shifting position, disappearing and reappearing in different configurations as he travels along a winding road sitting next to Dr Percepied's coachman. When we read this passage primed with a knowledge of trends in visual art of the period, it seems that Proust's prose is seeking similar ends to those of Cézanne in his later work and of the Cubist painters that came after him. Paul Cézanne (1839–1906) inaugurated a move away from conventional perspective in painting in the 1880s and 1890s ('he broke up consistent linear perspective with multiple perspectives, he violated aerial perspective in landscapes by painting objects in the distance as bright or brighter than those in the foreground'[14]), and this experimentation opened the way for later artists – such as Georges Braque and Pablo Picasso – radically to explore how our perception of physical objects could be depicted on the flat plane of a canvas. Multiple aspects of a single object were represented at once, as if fractured and multiplied by the perceiving conscience, and different objects on the same plane were depicted with different intensities, their boundaries fluid and indeterminate.

At the same time, the passage can be taken to illustrate the philosophical notion of perspectivism – the contention that there is no single truth but a multiplicity of truths, as many as there are ways of seeing – that has its roots in Nietzsche's writings. Proust and his ex-classmates from Condorcet showed a great deal of interest in Nietzsche's work in their short-lived journal *Le Banquet*. In successive numbers they published translated extracts from his writings and discussions of criticism of these works. The prefatory remarks to the journal's first number, signed collectively 'La redaction' [the editors], make intriguing reading. Proust, Gregh *et al.* are driven, they say, not just by a desire to see their own writings published, but also 'by the desire to make known in France, in a somewhat coherent manner, the most interesting and most recent productions of foreign art'.[15] Beyond the Martinville episode we find numerous instances in the *Search* of an individual or a state of affairs being described by the Narrator and then subsequently being recalled by other characters who display quite different conceptions of the reality or truth of what they recall. The questions raised in such moments about the relative value of truth and the nature (and fallibility) of perception are important for the novel's exploration of the key themes of time, memory and the status of the subject in relation to the material world.

A thinker whose writing also finds echoes in the Martinville episode is Henri Bergson (1859–1941), philosopher, public intellectual, cousin of Proust by marriage in 1891 and winner of the Nobel Prize for Literature in 1927. Bergson's conception of '*durée*' (time as subjectively experienced *duration*, rather than as measured by science), his interest in the nature of memory, its role in perception, and in the relation between mind and body, have led critics to speak of his influence on Proust's novel. In his metaphors for the interconnections between sensations, brain and body, Bergson often seems Proustian: the brain is 'a sort of central telephone exchange' and the sense organs are 'an immense keyboard, on which the material object executes all of a sudden its chord of a thousand notes'.[16] Doubtless the intersections, as well as the divergences, of many of Proust's key notions with Bergson's philosophy can be instructive, but it is important not to overplay the notion of influence or borrowing. Proust grants memory recall its pivotal position in his aesthetics in his notes for *Jean Santeuil* in 1895, and the *Carnet de 1908* indicates that he did not read Bergson's *Matter and Memory* (1896) until 1909.

Another figure pondering similar problems in the same period, this time primarily in the field of psychology, and whose thinking offers us a link between

Proust and his modernist contemporaries such as Joyce and Woolf, is William James (1842–1910). 'Consciousness does not appear to itself chopped up in bits', wrote James in 1890. 'It is nothing jointed; it flows … In talking of it hereafter, let us call it the stream of thought, of consciousness.'[17] James's conception of consciousness as a constant flux or flow finds its most forceful literary manifestations in Molly Bloom's monologue in Joyce's *Ulysses* (1922) and Woolf's *Mrs Dalloway* (1925). Throughout the *Search*, although much of the narrative comes to us directly from the thoughts and perceptions – the consciousness – of the first-person Narrator, things are further complicated by Proust's handling of chronology. We remain always close to the Narrator's thoughts, but the points from which he recounts his story vary: now he is a weary adult looking back on his life; now he is the young boy of Combray, in need of his mother's goodnight kiss; now a naive young man starting out in salon society. As we follow the Narrator through the *Search* we may be privy to the heady flux of his consciousness as James identified it and that Joyce and Woolf exposed in their own radical ways, but combining the non-linear chronology of the novel with the endless curiosity and critical sharpness of the Narrator's gaze, packaged elegantly in the surges and sinews of his prose, Proust proves that there are more things in the *Search* than were dreamt of in James's psychology.

A landmark of the period that I would like to consider in conclusion is the phenomenon that were the Ballets russes [Russian Ballets], brought to tour in Europe under the directorship of Sergei Diaghilev from 1909 to 1929. Proust's twin loves of music and theatre were satisfied by the lavish productions that showcased dancers such as Vaslav Nijinsky, Ida Rubenstein and Anna Pavlova. Proust greatly admired Wagner's operas, conceived as *Gesamtkunstwerk*s (total works of art), often taking several days to perform. The Ballets russes offered a quite different spectacle in terms of pace, duration and intensity; they did share, however, the totalizing ambition of Wagner's operas, albeit on a smaller scale. They brought together the foremost composers of the time, Debussy, Stravinsky, Satie and Ravel, with sumptuous sets and costumes by avant-garde artists and designers, amongst them Léon Bakst, Henri Matisse and Coco Chanel. In 1917 Proust attended a performance of *Parade*, a new ballet with a scenario written by Jean Cocteau, music by Éric Satie, sets and costumes by Picasso and programme notes by Guillaume Apollinaire. Proust's passion for music had led him, the previous year, to pay a string quartet to play works by Beethoven, Franck and Fauré for him as he lay in bed, an enraptured audience of one. He now had the apotheosis of high art before him on the stage of the Théâtre du Châtelet: art that challenged conventions, crossed boundaries and evinced the remarkable multiplier effect that collaboration across different media could have in the artistic sphere. This dynamic interplay is transposed into Proust's novel where the language and techniques of different art forms are used metaphorically as a sort of multiplier that enriches our understanding of the objects of the Narrator's and others' attention. Seen through a painter's eyes the statuary of the Balbec church is read like an illustrated bible; Elstir's paintings offer the Narrator (and his readers) a model of the functioning and structure of metaphor; the minutest detail of Vermeer's *View of Delft* offers the dying Bergotte momentary recognition of how he should have written his novels; and listening to Vinteuil's bewitching, previously unknown septet alerts the Narrator to the profound sensitivity and vision of the unassuming piano teacher whom he imagines like Michelangelo, having painted the sublime strokes of his 'musical fresco' with 'wild joy' (*C*, 287; *P*, 1794).

When we consider the relation of Proust's novel to the contexts or currents that fed into its production we become more aware of his tendency towards multiplication. Private events are lived through, then they come back, remembered. Real individuals lend character traits to fictional ones then go on to appear all the same alongside them in the fiction. References to real paintings, symphonies and poems spill out of the novel yet still there is space in it for imagined memoirs, paintings that have hung on no wall and musical phrases all the more haunting for their never having been inked on to a score. This proliferation is found at the level of language too, of course: characterizing the *Search* in 1929, Walter Benjamin wrote of 'the Nile of language, which here overflows and fructifies the regions of truth'.[18] On our low days as readers we might well wish for drought, or wish our author had been rather more parsimonious in his planning and plotting. But this is not gratuitous volume for volume's sake. Proust's was the age of mechanical reproduction yet there is nothing mechanistic about the proliferation we find in his novel. As Chapter Four will show, the dimensions of the novel and the material it draws within its compass are commensurate with its ambition – and ultimately its success – in charting the Narrator's long and uncertain passage towards his vocation.

Chapter 3

Early works and late essays

Running counter to Proust's tendency towards proliferation, popular conceptions of the man and his work are often decidedly reductive. 'Proust' more often than not means *madeleines*, means memory, means *In Search of Lost Time* or, in its older, Shakespearean guise, *Remembrance of Things Past*. The *Search*, of course, is Proust's *magnum opus*, his major contribution to world literature and to European literary culture, and it is quite right that he should be remembered for it. Voluminous, even encyclopaedic, as it is, however, the *Search* is not Proust's only work. He committed the last fourteen years of his life to it, the *summa* of a lifetime's thinking, but its outline did not materialize from nowhere. This chapter offers an overview of Proust's works before the *Search*, showing how his sensibilities developed as a writer and how his early writings bear traces of interests and preoccupations that develop more fully in the *Search*. I keep in focus Proust's near-constant vacillation between different literary forms in his early years, his many experiments with literary style and his tireless scrutiny (and often scathing analysis) of society life. The main works are surveyed in chronological order of their composition.

Pleasures and Days

Proust's first book was neither a commercial nor a critical success. Its title was suggestive of dilettantism and idle leisure, in contrast to Hesiod's *Works and Days* on which it riffs; it was a luxury edition, whose price was four times the average cost of a book at the time; and its presentation – prefaced somewhat enigmatically by Anatole France, illustrated by society hostess Madeleine Lemaire and including four pieces for piano by Reynaldo Hahn – meant that the audience to whom it appealed was small from the start. Proust's decision to send dedicated copies to many individuals who might otherwise have bought it meant that sales were even lower than he might have hoped.

Although many of the pieces in the collection had already been published in *Le Banquet*, *La Revue blanche* and elsewhere, *Pleasures and Days* is far more than a 'collected juvenilia'.[1] It has a subtle architecture: there are carefully orchestrated shifts between the serious (the tale of a dying man wracked by jealousy, 'The Death of Baldassare Silvande', opens the collection), the light-hearted (such as the 'Fragments from Italian Comedy' that draw implicit parallels between the *Commedia dell'arte* and the role-play of the Parisian social scene) and the downright funny (see the pastiche 'Bouvard and Pécuchet on Society and Music', where Flaubert's fictional copyists ponder entering society). We switch between unrequited love ('Mme de Breyves's Melancholy Summer Vacation') and the promise and pleasure of art, as explored in the 'Portraits of Painters and Musicians', poems inspired by the work of artists Proust had admired at the Louvre (all from the seventeenth century: the Dutchmen Albert Cuyp and Paul Potter, the French painter and engraver Antoine Watteau and the Flemish painter and portraitist Antoine Van Dyck) and by four favourite composers. The latter are from the eighteenth and nineteenth centuries: Chopin, Gluck, Schumann and Mozart. After the poems come 'The Confession of a Young Woman', a substantial, psychologically fraught tale of moral trauma and suffering, followed by a lighter prose piece, 'A Dinner in Town'; then come a series of short prose poems, 'Nostalgia – Daydreams under Changing Skies', which consider emotions, landscapes and fleeting scenarios of various sorts. The original, wistful title, 'Les regrets, rêveries couleur du temps', incorporates a characteristically Proustian play on '*le temps*', the word for time and for the weather. Time passing and reflection on the past are concerns of these pieces which have much, stylistically, to identify them with the literary currents of their time. The collection ends with a novella, grave in tone and purpose, entitled 'The End of Jealousy'.

Besides the vanities and vicissitudes of society life the dominant concerns of the collection are the joys and, more prominently, the sufferings of love; jealousy; habit; the passing of time; memory; contingency; and death, which brings the first and the last stories to their glum conclusions. All of these preoccupations will eventually take their place, to varying degrees of prominence, in the *Search*.

Various traits of *Pleasures and Days* distinguish it from the later novel. Most obviously perhaps, at the centre of the collection we find the poetic 'Portraits of Painters and Musicians'. The Narrator of the *Search* frequently refers to poets, major and minor, but nowhere does verse of his own appear. The 'Portraits' are largely derivative, echoing Baudelaire's 'Les Phares' [The Beacons] in which each of the first eight stanzas is dedicated to a tutelary artist figure (Rubens, Da Vinci and others). For all the apparent divergence between the brevity and intensity of the poetic line and the slower-paced unfolding of the Proustian sentence in the *Search*, that poems commemorating artists should form the core of *Pleasures and Days* shows us how early Proust came to revere art and to explore the responses that great art elicits. Many of the pieces on either side of the poems show the vanity and illusion – the 'temps perdu' – that society life represents. Proust's poems may lack originality but they underline his recognition of the crucial importance of solitary contemplation and reflection, so markedly different from the buzz and bustle of social interaction.

An aspect of the collection that dates it rather as a work of the nineteenth century is the decadent style and tone of certain passages, reminiscent of writers such as Huysmans, author of *Against Nature* (1884), whose protagonist Des Esseintes lives a life of artificial pleasures, withdrawn from society and the natural world. In 'Fragments from Italian Comedy' we read of one character 'unstopping a small bottle and explaining ... that he has formed a concentrate of the most potent and most exotic perfumes' (*PD*, 53; *PJ*, 51). Shortly after, we read of another, echoing the extravagances of Montesquiou, 'describing his new bedroom, skilfully treated with tar to evoke the sensations of a sea voyage, and ... detailing ... all the quintessences of his dressing table and his furnishings' (*PD*, 53, trans. mod.; *PJ*, 52). Proust's text shows his sensitivity to the currents of his time and his talent in reproducing their traits with a very few choice phrases. We find the same practice in the later pastiches, of which 'Bouvard and Pécuchet on Society and Music' in *Pleasures and Days* provides a satirical foretaste.

Proust's first book serves as a seedbed for stylistic practices, themes, images and scenarios that are developed in his subsequent writings. Involuntary memory, the best known of Proust's fascinations, features with some regularity in the collection, although without the same impact it has for the Narrator in the *Search*. The dying Baldassare Silvande hears the sound of distant bells on the breeze that enters his sickroom: 'it was a voice both present and very ancient', we read as the bells remind him of crossing the fields in the evening, heading home as a young boy (*PD*, 27; *PJ*, 27). In 'Mme de Breyves's Melancholy Summer Vacation' the heroine longs for a man she has fallen for but who escapes her grasp. Hearing again a phrase from *Die Meistersinger*, heard the night they first met, 'had the capacity to evoke M. de Laléande for her with the greatest precision' (*PD*, 77; *PJ*, 74). 'She had involuntarily turned [the phrase] into the real leitmotif of M. de Laléande', we are told (*PD*, 77; *PJ*, 74): this anticipates Swann and Odette's relation, in which the little phrase from Vinteuil's sonata, heard the night they first met, becomes for Swann the mnemonic embodiment of his love for Odette, the 'national anthem of their love' (*SW*, 262; 180).

Besides early indications of Proust's recognition of the affective potential of involuntary memory, we also find in *Pleasures and Days* fledgling forms of certain images and motifs. In 'Fragments from Italian Comedy' the Narrator speaks of a character called Hippolyta whose sons and nephews 'like her, all have aquiline noses, thin lips, piercing eyes, and over-delicate skin' in which he recognizes 'traces of her lineage, which doubtless issued from a goddess and a bird' (*PD*, 43–4; *PJ*, 42–3). In *The Guermantes Way*, this genealogical image returns, refined:

> The features of the Duchesse de Guermantes, … the nose like a falcon's beak, the piercing eyes, seemed to have served also as a pattern for … Robert's face … I looked longingly at those features of his so character-istic of the Guermantes, of that race which … seemed to have sprung, in the age of mythology, from the union of a goddess with a bird.
> (*G*, 84–5; 807)

Readers will find many such instances of *Pleasures and Days* serving as a test-ing ground for Proust's pen: the cherished goodnight kiss features in 'The Confession of a Young Woman'; in the Flaubert pastiche the Jews are described as forming 'a sort of vast secret society, like the Jesuits and the Freemasons' (*PD*, 64; *PJ*, 62), terms which recur almost verbatim to describe homosexuals in *Sodom and Gomorrah*. The clinching 'meeting by the lakeside' in 'Nostalgia – Daydreams under Changing Skies' is a contingent moment of misinterpret-ation, similar to when in *The Guermantes Way* Saint-Loup, passing in an open carriage at Doncières, apparently feigns not to recognize the Narrator. In the earlier piece we see Proust's recognition of the force of the mind in convincing us of the reality of states of affairs that are only ever figments of our imagin-ation. 'The most horrible thing about my mistake', the protagonist reflects, 'was that it refused to go away' (*PD*, 129; *PJ*, 124), anticipating the Narrator's agon-izing in *The Captive* over Albertine, fuelled more by his ever-active mind than by any hard proof of wrongdoing.

It is instructive to consider the image of society that emerges from *Pleasures and Days*. Proust was initially taken for little more than a fawning socialite but reading the collection shows us in fact how clear-sighted he was from an early age about the reality of high society. Violante explains to her family servant why she speaks about things she formerly despised: 'I would be less popular if I expressed preoccupations which, by their very superiority, are neither liked nor understood by people in high society' (*PD*, 35; *PJ*, 35). Why, we might ask, with this awareness, is she not able to escape? Because, writes Proust with remarkable maturity (the story is dated August 1892), of the force of *habit*, 'a force which, if it is nourished at first by vanity, vanquishes weariness, contempt, and even boredom' (*PD*, 38, trans. mod.; *PJ*, 37). For the protagonist of 'The Confession of a Young Woman', society is a place where vice is easily indulged, characterized by the 'plaisirs déssechants' [dessicating pleasures] it offers (*PD*, 95; *PJ*, 90). And the socialites in 'The Death of Jealousy', like Mme Verdurin eating her croissant as she reads about the sinking of the *Lusitania* (*TR*, 102; 2190), pay lip service to a fellow *mondain*'s suffering 'while they swallow a last glass of champagne ... sensing, from the pleasure they derived from drinking it, that "*they* were in an excellent way"' (*PD*, 163; *PJ*, 158). Proust's vision of society life and people is neither sycophantic nor snobbish here; he cuts through the trappings of privilege and knocks holes through the gleaming surfaces to expose the empty centre of *le beau monde*. The collection contains many promising and beautifully crafted miniatures, but it would take over ten more years for the grander structures of the mature novel to coalesce.

Jean Santeuil

It is likely that it was in September 1895, during a trip with Reynaldo Hahn to Sarah Bernhardt's summer retreat at Belle-Île-en-Mer off the Britanny coast and to Beg-Meil on the mainland, that Proust began work on drafts for a novel that he never finished, entitled by its first, posthumous editor *Jean Santeuil*. To call it a novel is already an overstatement: Proust's notes are fragmentary, frequently contradictory and lacking in unifying structure. In mid September 1896 Proust explained that he had written over 100 pages of his project but was still not able 'to conceive of its totality'.[2] *Jean Santeuil* was first published in 1952 in three volumes edited by Bernard de Fallois, who pieced the 'novel' together from 1,500 pages of notes by moving passages around, omitting sections, amalgamating disparate ones, modifying and suppressing names and details as he saw fit, ultimately compiling ten thematic sections organized according to the apparent age of the protagonist. In 1971 the material was re-edited for the *Bibliothèque de la Pléiade*. Although the *Pléiade* editors acknowledge the unfinished nature of the text, their editorial interventions, like those of Fallois, give a greater impression of cohesion and uniformity than is in fact evinced by the materials themselves. In an unfinished introductory note, Proust wrote 'Should I call this book a novel? It is something less, perhaps, and yet much more, the very essence of my life, with nothing extraneous added'.[3] And this is precisely the issue: the fragments that make up *Jean Santeuil* represent a store of raw materials harvested from Proust's personal experience, but they are not yet bound together coherently by plot, structure and pacing, crucial elements that define the novelist's craft.

Proust began with a frame narrative in which two friends meet an author, 'C…', who gives them a manuscript, the story of Jean Santeuil, which they publish when its author dies. Many characters and events that first take shape in the *Jean Santeuil* notes can be found in similar or transposed forms in the *Search*. Jean's fictional friend Henri de Réveillon, for example, may be seen as an early version of Robert de Saint-Loup, and Jean shares many traits with the Narrator of the *Search*. Jean wants to be an artist: he seeks 'an opportunity of concentrating my mind, of digging deep into myself, of trying to find out the truth of things, of expressing the whole of myself, of occupying myself with what is genuine, and not … essentially futile' (*JS*, 191; 440). An important development is the recognition of the power of involuntary memory as a potential route to revelation for the artist or potential artist. Memories of time spent by the sea are revived in Jean as he looks out over Lake Geneva: the sudden intrusion of an unexpected memory, he realizes, 'nous attache définitivement à la vie et nous l'incorpore' [attaches us firmly to life and makes it part of us] (*JS*, 407, trans. mod.; 399). Anticipating the role of involuntary memory in the *Search*, Jean recognizes such moments as

> the happy hours of the poet's life when chance has set upon his road a sensation which holds within itself a past, which promises the imagination that it shall make contact with a past it never knew, which never came within the range of its vision, which no amount of intelligence, effort or desire could ever have made it know. (*JS*, 408; 399)

In *Jean Santeuil* we also find other familiar scenarios, such as the goodnight kiss; childhood reading; the discovery that the family cook's culinary brilliance is tempered by brutality and sadism towards the kitchen maid; scenes of jealous snooping and suffering; and a little phrase from a sonata by Saint-Saëns whose affective powers anticipate those attributed to Vinteuil's sonata in the *Search*. In the previous chapter we saw how political affairs are generally viewed in the *Search* through the optic of society conversation and not explored as events of interest in their own right. Some of the fragments of *Jean Santeuil* show that this approach was arrived at after the more conventional tactic of working through the ins and outs of political intrigues had been tried and rejected. *Jean Santeuil* contains lengthy notes on the Dreyfus Affair, in particular Zola's trial, which Jean attends religiously, and a semi-fictionalized account of an influential government minister compromised by the 1892 Panama Canal scandal.

Proust's syntax in the *Jean Santeuil* notes is not as confidently expansive and elastic as it is in the *Search*: we can see him testing his range, often reaching dead-ends. His analytical eye and his taste for metaphoric elaboration are clearly maturing but the drafts were abandoned before a coherent whole could take shape. Before Proust could make the critical transition from the third-person narrative of 'Jean' to the clinching '*Je*' of the mature novel, there were still several developmental stages for him to travel.

Ruskin

Proust discovered the work of John Ruskin (1819–1900) most likely through Paul Desjardins, a professor at the School of Political Sciences, and through his reading of Robert de la Sizeranne's *Ruskin et la religion de la beauté* [*Ruskin and the Religion of Beauty*] (1897). Ruskin's death in 1900 spurred French public interest in the man and his work and Proust capitalized on this, publishing a number of articles as well as heavily annotated translations of *The Bible of Amiens* in 1904 and *Sesame and Lilies* in 1906. *Sesame and Lilies* (1865) is one of Ruskin's most popular works, combining two lectures, the first discussing reading, the second considering the education of women; the 'bible' of Amiens is a metaphor for the city's cathedral, of which Ruskin's book (1885) is an architectural appraisal and celebration. In his preface to *The Bible of Amiens*, while expressing admiration for Ruskin, Proust also takes his distance, identifying in Ruskin's thinking a tendency towards taking pleasure from erudition rather than from a purer, less egotistical celebration of the beauty of a work of art in its own right. Proust terms this *idolatry* – 'an infirmity essential to the human mind' (*ASB*, 187; *CSB*, 134); it was a potential pitfall he sought to avoid thereafter in his own writings. The important preface to Proust's *Sesame and Lilies* anticipates many of the major themes and some key scenarios of 'Combray' and of the *Search* more generally.[4] Proust worked closely with his mother and Reynaldo Hahn's cousin Marie Nordlinger on the translations: the two women provided working glosses of Ruskin's English, which Proust then elaborated and reworked, creating a remarkably rich and fluid French text. Immersing himself in Ruskin taught Proust how to see, charged the universe with 'infinite value' (*ASB*, 191; *CSB*, 139) and led him yet nearer to his own creative aesthetics.

Pastiches

Pleasures and Days contained an entertaining pastiche of Flaubert's celebrated novel *Bouvard and Pécuchet*. The Lemoine Affair offered Proust his subject matter for a series of further pastiches published to great acclaim in *Le Figaro* in February and March 1908 (see Chapter One above for a summary of the affair). This creative exercise, replicating aspects of style and technique characteristic of the voice of other authors was a vital step in Proust's development as a writer. The pastiches demonstrate brilliantly Proust's ear for the particular music of an author's prose style, his eye for motifs, tics or favoured structures. His virtuosity is evident in the range of authors and genres he takes on: he offers accounts of the affair with the exhaustive socio-historical chronicling of Balzac, the tense impersonality of Flaubert, and offers an imaginary critique of the latter piece as if written by Sainte-Beuve. He recreates the voices of recent and contemporary writers Ernest Renan, Henri de Régnier, the Goncourt brothers in their journal (a brilliant pastiche of the Goncourt journal, chronicling a dinner *chez* Verdurin, features, of course, in *Time Regained*: see *TR*, 23–32; 2140–6) and the critic and *Académicien* Emile Faguet. The more distant voices of the historian Jules Michelet and the Duc de Saint-Simon complete the set collected together in 1919 in *Pastiches et mélanges*. These pieces show Proust honing his craft as a writer and expose the sense of humour, often overlooked, that subtends so much of the *Search*. Looking back, Proust described the exercise as 'a matter of hygiene; … necessary to purge oneself of the most natural vice of idolatry and imitation'.[5] He thought it better consciously to perform a parody and then move on than risk spending a lifetime writing involuntary imitations of revered forebears. He described his pastiches as 'literary criticism "in action"'.[6] That he should envisage his instinctive, creative endeavours as a form of criticism points towards the lack of rigid generic divisions in his thinking: this fluidity would become all the more apparent in the subsequent writings we know as *Against Sainte-Beuve*, the abandoned hybrid project from which the great novel would grow.

Against Sainte-Beuve

Although the published editions suggest otherwise, like *Jean Santeuil*, the writings known as *Against Sainte-Beuve* are fragmentary and unfinished. They are, however, extremely valuable for the insight they offer into the development of Proust's aesthetics since, like the earlier essay 'Against Obscurity', they provide an opportunity to see Proust functioning as critic. They also show him trying out and refining material that was subsequently incorporated into the *Search*. In a letter of May 1908, in an eclectic list of works in progress, including 'a Parisian novel', 'an essay on pederasty' and 'an article on stained-glass', Proust mentioned 'an essay on Sainte-Beuve and Flaubert'.[7] This is the first of his mentioning a projected work relating to the critic. Six months later, it had still not taken material form. Proust told two correspondents that *in his mind* he had constructed an article on Sainte-Beuve in two different forms: one classical essay and one more narrative in style, where his mother arrives at his bedside and he proceeds to tell her about an article on Sainte-Beuve that he intends to write.[8] When he eventually put pen to paper in the *Carnet de 1908* and elsewhere, the notes and drafts that he made show that he never definitively made his mind up with regard to the generic nature of the project: some of the critical pieces bear traces of the envisaged dialogue form and different editions of *Against Sainte-Beuve* give varying impressions of the balance between critical essay and fictional development. The material was first edited by Fallois in 1954. This edition includes a good deal of Proust's sketches that are in fact early drafts for the *Search*, and not therefore strictly related to Sainte-Beuve. This edition is still published in the Folio 'Essais' collection. In 1971 the text was re-edited for the *Bibliothèque de la Pléiade* by Pierre Clarac, who excised the purely fictional material and focused uniquely on the fragments of the abandoned critical essay.

Against Sainte-Beuve is something of a miscellany, then, encompassing critical reflection and appraisal, novelistic drafts and theoretical passages on the nature of memory, creativity and art. Proust's half-dozen pages of draft prefatory material are a case in point and are fascinating, highly recommended reading. Here we find the description of a succession of moments of involuntary memory that will become pivotal in the *Search* (at this stage toast, rather than *madeleine*, is dunked in tea). They are worked through in support of the crucial reflection that sensation is to be prized over intellect, since memories conjured by contingent sensory stimuli can put us in touch with 'the intimate essence of ourselves' (*ASB*, 7; *CSB*, 215) in a way that active intellectual endeavour cannot. Proust recognizes the problem of setting out this position in writing, itself reliant on the intelligence, but he maintains that humility and the highest artistic achievements will come from intelligently acknowledging the inferiority of the intelligence. The prefatory notes, like several of the other pieces in the collection, are only loosely related to Sainte-Beuve but are directly concerned with setting out Proust's own theory of literature.

The piece entitled 'Sainte-Beuve's Method' is vital for our understanding what Proust's projected essay was responding to. Charles-Augustin Sainte-Beuve (1804–69), one of the nineteenth century's most influential critics, believed that in order best to understand and appreciate a writer it was necessary to inform oneself about his (Sainte-Beuve's subjects were predominantly male) behaviour in society, his finances, his diet, his vices, his daily routine. Proust argues, however, that 'such a method fails to recognize what any more than merely superficial acquaintance with ourselves teaches us: that a book is the product of a self other than that which we display in our habits, in company, in our vices' (*ASB*, 12; *CSB*, 221–2). That Sainte-Beuve should chose to judge writers on the basis of their social selves, which bear no relation to the deeper selves that produce their art, is proof for Proust that the revered critic lacked a true understanding of artistic creativity – of literature itself – which he placed on the same plane as conversation. Sainte-Beuve's weekly column in *Le Constitutionnel* was entitled 'Causeries' (talk or chatter), something quite opposed to the silence and withdrawal Proust believed to be necessary for the production of art.

Proust's own skills as a gifted and sensitive close reader are greatly in evidence in his critical pieces on Nerval, Balzac, Flaubert and Baudelaire; they do offer, however, a rather unusual reading experience because of their hybridity. In the essay 'Sainte-Beuve and Balzac', for instance, we find a sudden switch from the critical discussion to a fictional scenario played out in support of the point being made. Proust argues that 'We come closer to an understanding of the great men of antiquity if we understand them as Balzac did than if we understand them like Sainte-Beuve'; two lines later he writes:

> Balzac … like other novelists … had an audience of readers who did not ask that his novels should be works of literature, merely ones interesting for their imaginings and observations. What held them was not his faults of style but rather his virtues and his researches. In the little library on the second floor whither, on Sundays, M. de Guermantes hurried to take refuge at the first ring of the doorbell from his wife's callers … he had the whole of Balzac, bound in gilded calf with labels of green leather. (*ASB*, 70–1; *CSB*, 278–9)

This sort of unannounced shift shows us quite how intermingled were Proust's various projects announced as 'under way' in mid 1908. In August 1909 he approached the editor Alfred Vallette, telling him that he was

> finishing a book which, despite its provisional title, *Contre Sainte-Beuve: souvenir d'une matinée* [*Against Sainte-Beuve, Memory of a Morning*], is a real novel and one which is extremely indecent in places. One of the main characters is a homosexual … The book ends with a long conversation on Sainte-Beuve and on aesthetics … and when you finish it, you'll see, I hope, that the whole novel is but a putting into action of the principles of art that are expressed in that final part, a sort of preface if you like placed at the end.[9]

These comments show how in the space of a year Proust moved from a projected critical essay through a phase of simultaneous creative and critical compositions to a point where he was comfortable with calling his work to date 'a real novel'. A developed Charlus narrative was evidently present in Proust's working drafts at this stage, but in a way that is not clearly distinct from the critical project. The idea of having a theoretical discussion that closes the work whilst exposing the principles of art that have guided its development is one that is carried over to *Time Regained* where the Narrator, in the Prince de Guermantes' library, reflects on his experiences and holds forth on the nature of the work of art he hopes to produce, founded on those experiences. *Against Sainte-Beuve*, then, is the final, transitional stage between Proust's extended search for a voice and a form and his embarking on the novel proper. Two final pieces should detain us before we consider in detail each of the volumes of the *Search* in turn.

Late essays

Despite his ill health and endless corrections and revisions to the manuscripts and proofs of the *Search*, in the post-war years Proust still, from time to time, had letters and other pieces published in newspapers and journals. The essays 'A propos du "style" de Flaubert' [On Flaubert's Style] and 'A propos de Baudelaire' [Concerning Baudelaire], published as letters to the editor in the *Nouvelle Revue Française* (*NRF*) in January 1920 and June 1921 respectively, merit attention not only for their critical insights but also for what they reveal of Proust's artistic commitment, his writerly methods, the capaciousness and elasticity of his thinking. The Flaubert essay responds to comments made in the *NRF* by critic Albert Thibaudet, suggesting that Flaubert was not a first-rate writer to whom verbal mastery came naturally. The Baudelaire piece marked the poet's centenary. In both essays (which draw on material first developed in the *Against Sainte-Beuve* drafts), Proust's approach is unconventional, indirect and extremely effective. 'It is not that I love Flaubert's books, or even Flaubert's style above all others' (*ASB*, 261; *CSB*, 586), he writes, before going on to anatomize and celebrate Flaubert's stylistic and grammatical singularities. As for Baudelaire, although Proust avers him to be, with Vigny, the greatest poet of the nineteenth century, a number of pages are spent praising Hugo and Vigny before the chosen subject is properly addressed. Once we have navigated these circuitous beginnings we come to realize that what Proust appreciates in his notorious forebears illuminates what is most important in his own art. To read Proust on the positioning and function of adverbs and prepositions in Flaubert is to recognize the care and the musical finesse with which Proust's own finely spun phrases were formed. To read him privileging over Hugo's bombast 'what poor Baudelaire found in the suffering intimacy of his own heart and body' (*ASB*, 296–7; *CSB*, 628) reinforces for us how much of his own writing stems from the extended, painful dialogue between his fervently productive mind and its ever-diminishing corporeal envelope.

In the Flaubert essay Proust, now the established novelist who has his own, assured voice, recommends 'the purgative and exorcising merits of pastiche' to budding writers struck with 'l'intoxication flaubertienne' [Flaubert-poisoning] (*ASB*, 268; *CSB*, 598). Moreover, he uses his corrective to Thibaudet's misreading of Flaubert to correct misapprehensions of his own work. Certain readers of *Swann's Way* had failed to recognize what Proust terms 'its rigorous though veiled structure', dismissing it as merely a 'collection of memories, their sequence determined by the fortuitous laws of the association of ideas'. Proust responds to this 'counter-truth' by arguing that 'in order to move from one plane on to another plane, I had simply made use not of a fact, but of what I had found to be purer and more precious as a junction, a phenomenon of memory' (*ASB*, 273; *CSB*, 599). He goes on to trace the lineage of this structural use of involuntary recollection to Chateaubriand and to Nerval. In 'Concerning Baudelaire' he does something similar in exploring Baudelaire's unfulfilled desire to entitle the collection that became *Les Fleurs du Mal* '*Les Lesbiennes*', who are 'as Baudelaire's aesthetic and moral conceptions would have it, "Flowers of Evil"' (*ASB*, 301; *CSB*, 632), this connection offering a link, which Proust expands upon, to their shared fascination with lesbianism. The essays that begin, then, as a defence of Flaubert and a celebration of Baudelaire undoubtedly achieve their goals with great elegance and critical acuity; but they function on a number of planes at once, proving, in fact, also to be the veiled attempts of a dying author, the publication of his life's work not yet complete, to align himself with major, controversial figures of the century into which he was born, before he is consigned to oblivion.

Chapter 4

In Search of Lost Time

Swann's Way

'Combray I' plunges us into the Narrator's reflections, looking back at his life, on sleep and consciousness, time, memory and identity. Then the focus shifts to the narrow segment of his childhood he can voluntarily recall, the period when his only consolation during the trauma of going to bed was his mother's kiss, often denied him when his parents had guests. Many years later, tasting a *madeleine* dipped in lime-blossom tea, the memory of the rest of his childhood in provincial Combray is suddenly restored to him. 'Combray II' tells of this life: we learn about the Narrator's family, their servant Françoise, their friend Charles Swann; we also glimpse the aristocratic Guermantes family and the Narrator's first indications of wanting to become an artist. 'Swann in Love', an interpolated tale told in the third person, moves back beyond the Narrator's childhood to recount Swann's troubled love affair with Odette de Crécy, one of the little clan of 'faithfuls' at the home of the Verdurins, a socially ambitious bourgeois couple. Swann also moves in the highest circles of society and we encounter some of the prominent figures at a soirée he attends, held by the Marquise de Sainte-Euverte. The final section, 'Place-names: The Name', begins with a discussion of the evocative power of place-names, before turning back to the time when the Narrator would play in the 'Champs-Élysées' with Swann's daughter Gilberte (first met in Combray). The Narrator loves Gilberte but soon she disappears, leaving him bereft. The volume closes with a passage, narrated from a much later point in time, reflecting on the irrevocable changes that have occurred in the Bois de Boulogne since that distant period of the Narrator's childhood. He sombrely acknowledges the unrelenting advance of time and the impossibility of holding on to, or voluntarily recreating, the past.

'Longtemps, je me suis couché de bonne heure' [For a long time I would go to bed early] (*SW*, 1; 13): thus with a phrase both awkward and banal we are drawn into Proust's novel. 'Longtemps', the adverb of duration that opens the French text does so with a backward glance towards a distant past. The verb that follows it, however, in the perfect tense, suggests a short-lived or one-off completed action with a closer relation to the present than 'longtemps' would normally suppose. No sooner do we start to wonder from where in time this voice speaks to us than it begins to ask similar questions about who, what and where it is. And from the seemingly childish admission of regular early nights we shift swiftly to the reflections of a reader of works on churches, chamber music and sixteenth-century history, unsure of his own position yet adept at drawing analogies to illustrate his uncertainty.

As this reading of the novel's opening paragraph shows at a micro-textual level and the summary of the volume above shows at a macro-textual one, *Swann's Way* has a challenging, non-linear structure. The slew of memories and reflections upon which we are cast adrift, however, in the first few pages, serves a vital purpose: we share the Narrator's uncertainty, like him we struggle to find our bearings. Announcing at the end of the opening pages that he 'used to spend the greater part of the night recalling [his] life in the old days at Combray …, at Balbec, Paris, Doncières, Venice' (*SW*, 8; 17), the Narrator is attributing names to the places in which the rooms he has been describing can be found: we have been given a brisk tour of the primary locations of the novel to come, rather like the rapid succession of inter-cut vignettes we are presented with in a movie trailer.

After this unsettling swirl, we return to the Narrator's early childhood at Combray when the dread of bedtime was his primary fixation. His family seek to distract him with a magic lantern, a projector perched atop a lamp whose light casts images from slides on to his bedroom walls. This is the Narrator's first experience of the transformative and moral aspects of storytelling: the lantern brings lively colour and movement to his room's normally unremarkable walls; the story that flows across them is that of Geneviève de Brabant (a distant relative, we later learn, of Mme de Guermantes), sought out and abducted by the wicked Golo, whose crimes drive the sensitive young Narrator 'to a more than ordinarily scrupulous examination of [his] own conscience' (*SW*, 10; 18).

On the evenings when Charles Swann came to visit, the Narrator's mother's kiss would be withheld, leaving him inconsolable in his room, tortured by the sounds of his parents' conversation with Swann, 'the unwitting author of [his] sufferings' (*SW*, 50; 43). Thus Swann is introduced as a barrier to the Narrator's happiness. He is, of course, far more (Samuel Beckett described Swann as 'the corner-stone of the entire structure'[1]), but when we later learn quite how much Swann's own existence was blighted by despair relating to his love affair with Odette, it seems apt that his first role should be as a harbinger of suffering.

Because Swann's father during his lifetime was fond of the Narrator's grandfather, Swann still visits the family at Combray. Swann *père* was a stockbroker; Swann *fils*, however, is 'one of the most distinguished members of the Jockey Club, a particular friend of the Comte de Paris and of the Prince of Wales, and one of the men most sought after in the aristocratic world of the Faubourg Saint-Germain' (*SW*, 16; 22). He is discreet about his sparkling social connections, far-removed from the horizons of the Narrator's great aunts, but they suspect nothing since, as the Narrator puts it 'middle-class people in those days took what was almost a Hindu view of society, which they held to consist of sharply defined castes … from which nothing … could extract you and translate you to a superior caste' (*SW*, 16; 22–3). As the novel develops, individuals of almost every social station voice suspicion of *arrivistes*, and events show that marriage can elevate individuals to a new social circle but cannot guarantee their acceptance. At the same time, however, the *Search* tells of many movements up and down the social ladder that contradict any notion of rigidly governed social boundaries. Odette (whose marriage to Swann attracts disapproval from the Narrator's bourgeois family and Swann's aristocratic acquaintances alike), Bloch, the Verdurins and the Narrator, amongst others, ultimately far surpass their class origins. Their mobility reflects the shifting social morphology of the Third Republic.

A key episode of 'Combray I' is the account of the night the Narrator's mother stays in his room. Desperate for one more kiss, he waits for Swann's departure then throws himself at his mother when she comes upstairs. As he waits, his heart beats 'with terror and joy' (*SW*, 40; 37) and the tension between these emotions underpins the scene that follows. Everything he had hoped for – his mother's presence, her soothing voice, her kiss – is granted him, yet he cannot be fully happy for he realizes that the episode is unrepeatable. These complex moments combining fear, partially satisfied yearnings, enlightenment and disappointment provide vital lessons about temporality and desire, which shape his subsequent psychological development. The novel the mother reads to her agitated son brings an additional twist: George Sand's *François le Champi* (1848) is the tale of a foundling brought up by a miller and his kindly wife,

Madeleine; eventually hounded from the house by the cruel miller, François returns after the death of the latter and marries his adoptive mother. With this oedipal tale, inset in a scene that already suggests the transgression of conventional mother–son relations, the Narrator receives an ambiguous initiation into literature: he daydreams, his mother skips the love scenes, so his understanding is incomplete, it is a sensory *impression*, filtered through the calming sounds of his mother's voice. In *Time Regained* (*TR*, 239–40; 2275–6) the Narrator enjoys moments of delight upon encountering a copy of the same book in the Prince de Guermantes' library that stem not from memories stirred up by the text but from a sensory appreciation of the object itself.

Such was the trauma of his bedtimes and the emotional magnitude of the night just discussed that the adult Narrator feels 'as though all Combray had consisted of but two floors joined by a slender staircase, and as though there had been no time there but seven o' clock at night' (*SW*, 50; 44). Until, that is, his contingent encounter much later in life with a *madeleine* dipped in lime-blossom tea, an experience which stirs within him a sudden rush of 'exquisite pleasure' (*SW*, 51; 45). Just as forgotten words or names stubbornly refuse to reveal themselves to us when we will them to appear, taking more tea and cake provides no further insight: voluntary physical action is useless, as are his attempts to remember the movements of his mind at the moment he was overwhelmed. Slowly, something rising from a great depth starts or quivers within him (the French verb is '*tressaillir*'). Then the memory appears: his Aunt Léonie used to give him morsels of tea-soaked *madeleine* on Sunday mornings in Combray. The sight of the cakes was not sufficient to resurrect his past: this requires the more complex sensation of taste. 'When from a long-distant past nothing subsists', the Narrator explains,

> after the people are dead, after the things are broken and scattered, taste and smell alone, more fragile but more enduring, more immaterial, more persistent, more faithful, remain poised a long time, like souls, remembering, waiting, hoping, amid the ruins of all the rest; and bear unflinchingly, upon the tiny and almost impalpable drop of their essence, the immense structure of recollection ['l'édifice immense du souvenir']. (*SW*, 54, trans. mod.; 46)

And so memories of the rest of his childhood pour forth into the Narrator's mind, yielding the crucial realization through his body that his present does bear a relation of continuity to his past, that he is the same person in the *now* of narration as in the *then* of the events he remembers.

Readers are well advised to linger over these pages, since echoes and transposed fragments of the episode are to be found dispersed throughout the novel. A detailed familiarity with key moments such as this permits us better to recognize and appreciate the novel's constant through-flow of motifs and memories, the subtle allusions that bind disparate parts of the text together.

The church has a dominant position in the Combray topography and a vital symbolic role in the novel: the building is not just the centre of the provincial community, it is a place where past and present time intermingle. The Counts of Brabant lie buried beneath the flagstones and in the family chapel above them sit their ancestors, the present-day Guermantes, bathed in light filtering through the stained-glass windows that represent their forebears. This sense of duration and continuity makes the church for the Narrator 'an edifice occupying, so to speak, a four-dimensional space – the name of the fourth being Time' (SW, 71; 57). In the original text we catch an echo here between the 'edifice occupant ... un espace à quatre dimensions' and the 'edifice immense du souvenir' said to be founded on the sensation of taste in the *madeleine* scene quoted above. The right trigger permits the revelation of the edifice built within us by our past experience; the church is a tangible structure whose 'fourth dimension' offers a way of understanding how time can be embodied. When in *Time Regained* the Narrator comes to the realization that he can write, a cathedral features among the analogies he draws on to suggest how his novel will be constructed (TR, 432; 2390)

'Combray II' chronicles the habits and customs of the Narrator's family and their acquaintances. Aunt Léonie is an aged hypochondriac who no longer leaves her bedroom, from whose window she obsessively comments on what she sees, her limited perspective supplemented by reports from the outside provided by Françoise. Her existence is determined entirely by Habit, the daily and weekly routines on whose rhythm her life depends. Françoise has been in Léonie's service for many years and the Narrator's image of her 'framed in the small doorway ... like the statue of a saint in her niche' (SW, 61; 51) is in keeping with the (albeit superficial) religiosity of her mistress and communicates the child Narrator's view of Françoise as a paragon of virtue.

The scales fall from his eyes, however, when he witnesses her engaged in the less than saintly business of killing a recalcitrant chicken for the family table, her exertions accompanied by cries of 'Filthy creature!' Thus disabused of the illusion that a person might have a single, indivisible character, the Narrator begins to realize that Françoise's virtues 'concealed many of these kitchen tragedies, just as history reveals to us that the reigns of the kings and queens ... portrayed as kneeling with their hands joined in prayer in the windows of churches were stained by oppression and bloodshed' (SW, 145; 104). The image here is characteristically democratic: servants and sovereigns are as morally fallible as each other, an insight to which the Narrator returns elsewhere in the *Search*.

The 'Combray' sections of *Swann's Way*, then, combine fond reflection on old habits with, as so often in childhood, a recurring pattern of illusions being displaced by unexpected discoveries. Family conventions and common-places – Léonie's habits and her feud with Eulalie; the father's barometer readings; walks on the Guermantes Way when the weather is fine; lunching early on a Saturday – are sociological studies as well as valuable lessons in how our experience of time and space is far from constant or uniform.

Discoveries and part-revelations abound: an unannounced visit to his Uncle Adolphe acquaints the Narrator with the bewitching 'lady in pink' (*SW*, 92–3; 71), subsequently revealed to be Odette de Crécy (later Mme Swann), a meeting which causes a rift in the family. Legrandin's highly variable attitude to the Narrator's family, depending on whose company he is in, reveals his snobbery, a vice against which he disingenuously rails. Homosexuality and sadism are revealed at Montjouvain when the Narrator voyeuristically witnesses Mlle Vinteuil, the daughter of the old piano teacher, with her lover. And Mme de Guermantes, whose beauty and mystique the Narrator had woven in his mind around the syllables of her name, is revealed, after great anticipation, to be no more other-worldly than 'the wives of doctors and tradesmen', as the 'fiery little spot at the corner of her nose' deflatingly attests (*SW*, 210; 144).

These scenes introduce many of the novel's central characters and themes, which develop at different rates as the novel progresses. Questions of class distinctions, snobbery and social aspiration are further explored in 'Swann in Love' and given their fullest treatment in *The Guermantes Way*. The Montjouvain scene prepares the ground for the preponderant role that homosexuality will play in *Sodom and Gomorrah*, *The Captive* and *The Fugitive*. The intractable laws of attraction and desire that are sketched for us in action with the Narrator's sudden infatuation with the 'lady in pink' find an echo when, through the hedge at Tansonville, he first sets eyes on Gilberte Swann and 'falls in love' with her (*SW*, 169–70; 119); not until much later do we learn that the objects of desire in these scenes are in fact mother and daughter.

The lesson of reality not measuring up to the Narrator's anticipations, learnt on his first encounter with Mme de Guermantes, is repeatedly replayed with variations throughout the *Search* (in *Within a Budding Grove*, for example, with the Narrator's first, long-awaited trip to the theatre and when he first meets Bergotte after long admiring his books). 'Combray' yields much more than disappointment, however: many happy, instructive hours are spent reading; the joy of contemplating the flowering hawthorns is not something the Narrator fully understands, but it sharpens his alertness to the interaction of the senses and the remarkable complexity of the simplest of natural phenomena. His inability to articulate the pleasure he draws from his engagement with nature when out walking illuminates for him the 'discordance between our impressions and their habitual expression' (*SW*, 185–6; 129). The consequent realization that he must therefore 'endeavour to see more clearly into the sources of [his] rapture' (*SW*, 186; 129) effectively formulates the Narrator's central goal in the novel. We witness his earliest attempt at fulfilling it in the prose fragment composed after travelling in Doctor Percepied's carriage and experiencing the shifting perspectives on the bell towers of the Martinville and Vieuxvicq churches afforded him by the winding road and his elevated position next to the coachman. Through the use of metaphor and analogy he seeks to account for the mysterious pleasure of his experience but his natural indolence and lack of self-belief mean that after this isolated moment his career as a writer stalls.

'Swann in Love' tells of Swann's affair with Odette de Crécy. We meet the 'little clan' of regulars at the house of M. and Mme Verdurin, whose climb up the social ladder is an important strand of the novel's subsequent development. Odette does not move in the same exalted circles as Swann, nor is she his intellectual equal. *Chez* Verdurin, however, when they are together, Vinteuil's sonata for piano and violin is played, a piece of music which had enraptured Swann a year before, at the heart of which is a little phrase of five notes that, heard again, quite bewitches him, offering 'the possibility of a sort of rejuvenation' (*SW*, 252; 174). Swann's relation with Odette is coloured by the aesthetic promise of the rediscovered sonata and the little phrase becomes a metaphor for their love. Despite the vulgarity of the company *chez* Verdurin, Swann's attachment to Odette grows. He sees in her a likeness to Botticelli's portrait of Zipporah and keeps a reproduction of the work on his desk. Focused on these substitute figures, the sonata and the portrait, Swann's feelings for Odette develop to the point of obsession. He arrives one night at the Verdurins' after she has left and, desperate to see her, departs on a manic chase around Paris. The Narrator explains that such a rush of 'feverish agitation' is all it takes to convert an infatuation into something much longer lasting: love.

> It is not even necessary for that person [who provoked the agitation] to have attracted us, up till then, more than or even as much as others. All that was needed was that our predilection should become exclusive. And that condition is fulfilled when ... the quest for the pleasures we enjoyed in his or her company is suddenly replaced by an anxious, torturing need, whose object is the person alone, an absurd, irrational need which the laws of this world make it impossible to satisfy and difficult to assuage – the insensate, agonising need to possess exclusively. (*SW*, 277–8; 190)

This passage merits quotation in full for in expressing the conundrum facing Swann it also encapsulates the Narrator's dilemma in his later relation with Albertine and, in a nutshell, Proust's painful conception of love.

The Verdurins soon tire of Swann, deemed a bore because of his connections to high society (to which they have no access); they seek to make a match between Odette and the Comte de Forcheville, the dim-witted brother-in-law of Saniette, one of their regulars. It becomes harder for Swann to see Odette; her evasiveness and his growing suspicions combine to fuel jealous investigations (knocking on windows in the dark, opening mail addressed to others) that only send him deeper into despair, damaging his mental and physical health. Gradually, through his manipulation of language and imagery, Proust makes 'Swann in Love' a study of desire as pathology; eventually, inevitably, like a cancer, Swann's love becomes 'inoperable' (*SW*, 371–2; 249).

For a time, however, there seems to be hope: Swann admits to himself Odette's stupidity and the vulgarity of the little clan. He attends a soirée held by Mme de Sainte-Euverte, a glorious set piece of metaphor-driven portraiture and social observation. The company of old acquaintances is salutary: Swann's conversation with the Princesse des Laumes (Mme de Guermantes as she was then known; *SW*, 410–12; 273–5) brilliantly captures the confidences, witticisms and familiarity one finds in the repartee of long-acquainted equals; it shows us Swann back in his element and highlights a marked contrast with the Verdurin milieu. The remission from his ills is suddenly shattered, however, when Vinteuil's sonata is played and his feelings for Odette flood back through the affective channels opened up by the little phrase. Ruinously he renews his attentions, his inquisitions: has she had lesbian affairs? Two or three times, is the devastating response, the only answer he had not anticipated. But the human capacity for suffering is great and, sponge-like, Swann absorbs yet more. What we consider to be our love or our jealousy, we are told, 'is composed of an infinity of successive loves, of different jealousies, each of which is ephemeral, although by their uninterrupted multiplicity they give us the impression of continuity, the illusion of unity', (*SW*, 448; 297). This multiplicity, one of many Proust identifies at the heart of human affairs, is one with which the Narrator has to reconcile himself after Albertine's death in *The Fugitive*.

While for Swann it is too late ('Swann in Love' concludes with his painful realization that he has wasted years of his life on a woman who 'was not his type'), we might hope that the story's many lessons – regarding truth and morality, fidelity, jealousy, possessiveness and the possibility of satisfaction – would stand the Narrator in good stead in his own amorous adventures. In the later volumes, however, we realize time and again that the Narrator's anxieties, his suffering and distress have a flavour of familiarity: we have seen them in blueprint in the pages of 'Swann in Love'.

'Place-names: The Name' closes *Swann's Way*. The Narrator considers the distinctions between our experience of a place and the anticipations we have of it, which are often tied closely to the evocative power of place-names, words with enormous associative potential, particularly for a mind like the Narrator's.[2] Balbec is a place he longs to visit as a child, spurred by tales from Legrandin and Swann of its rugged beauty and Norman Gothic church. A promised vacation in Italy fills his mind with images relating to the names of Florence and Venice, Parma and Pisa, but ill health prohibits him from going and the journeys, and experiences of these places, remain confined to Stevenson's 'pleasant land of counterpane'. The narrowing of experiential possibilities imposed by the Narrator's ill health serves to swell his fascination with language, the signs that stand for unknown worlds, and his capacity for detailed scrutiny of whatever scraps of experience his condition affords him.

He does not travel to Italy, but whilst in Paris he plays in the Champs-Élysées with Gilberte, his dream of friendship born in the glimpse through the Tansonville hedge now fulfilled. Odette, now Swann's wife and Gilberte's mother, is much admired in the Champs-Élysées and the Bois de Boulogne, where the Narrator drags Françoise in order to catch a glimpse of Mme Swann's elegance as she strolls among the trees.

The closing pages of *Swann's Way* come to us from a much later chronological perspective. The Narrator speaks of leaving the 'closed room' he inhabits in Paris to go to Trianon via the Bois de Boulogne. Thus he brings into immediate proximity in the text two experiences of the same location at quite distinct periods of time – his early childhood and his adult life. The child, infatuated with the beauty and allure of his friend's mother, saw the Bois as a sort of enchanted garden; now the adult's sentiments and shift in pace introduce a tone reminiscent of Chet Baker's gentle melancholy: the thrill is gone. Motorcars have replaced carriages, women are no longer elegant but 'dreadful creatures' who 'hobble by beneath hats on which have been heaped the spoils of aviary or kitchen garden' (*SW*, 511; 341). The experience of the *madeleine* might have been able to revive the memories of part of his past, but the Narrator's painful realization in the final pages of *Swann's Way* is that it is fruitless actively to seek in reality the images of the mind, since reality constantly evolves; if our memories have a powerful, positive sheen this is precisely because they are *mental* constructs and not realities in themselves.

Within a Budding Grove

In 'Mme Swann at Home', Part One of *Within a Budding Grove*, Odette takes centre stage. Time has passed. The erotic aspect of the Narrator's relation with Gilberte matures. He frequents the Swann household, meeting the writer Bergotte, whose works in part introduced him to literature in Combray. The role of art develops in importance, held always in tension with social inter-action and expectations: the Narrator makes his long-awaited trip to see the actress Berma perform but is overwhelmed and disappointed; and Bergotte's appearance and persona seem out of keeping with his writings. Norpois, the diplomat, a colleague of the Narrator's father, encourages the prospect of a liter-ary career for the Narrator, but he repeatedly procrastinates. He visits a brothel with his friend Bloch. He renounces his relations with Gilberte but sees her out walking with a young man and is troubled by his emotional response. In Part Two, 'Place-names: The Place', he travels to Balbec with his grandmother and Françoise, with a view to improving his health. His excessive anticipations mean that the reality of Balbec is at first a disappointment. He becomes famil-iar with the intellectual aristocrat Robert de Saint-Loup and his uncle, the enigmatic Baron de Charlus. The Narrator and Saint-Loup meet the painter, Elstir, a key tutelary figure, whose studio resembles a laboratory for a new cre-ation of the world. Elstir introduces the Narrator to the band of young girls who add an unprecedented new dimension to his existence. Amongst them is Albertine Simonet, upon whom his scattered attentions ultimately converge. Balbec offers seemingly unlimited opportunities for exploration and discov-ery – sociological, intellectual, sexual – but Albertine refuses his kiss, the sea-son ends, the holiday-makers must part. He returns to Paris wiser to the world, charged with yet more curiosity, but little closer to fulfilling his vocation.

The French title *A l'ombre des jeunes filles en fleurs* has a strangeness (how can young girls be 'in flower' and who or what could be 'in their shadow'?) which is rather diluted in the English *Within a Budding Grove*.[3] Both titles, however, suggest organic growth and, perhaps more than any other, this volume gives a sense of genuine forward movement as we follow the Narrator's maturation in love and in matters of art and society. The part-revelations of *Swann's Way* filled him with a desire to 'see more clearly into the sources of [his] rapture' (*SW*, 186; 129), and in *Within a Budding Grove* there are further moments of fleeting exalt-ation which pique his sensibilities yet at this stage remain opaque: there is the 'cool, fusty smell' in the little pavilion in the Champs-Élysées (*BG*, 74; *JF*, 393); first hearing Vinteuil's sonata (*BG*, 118–22; *JF*, 422–5); seeing the sunrise from the train approaching Balbec (*BG*, 268; *JF*, 520–1); and the sight of a stand of trees at Hudimesnil (*BG*, 345; *JF*, 568). These experiences provide happiness and confusion in roughly equal measure: the Narrator's analysis of them is never satisfactorily completed since his roving attentions tend to stray elsewhere. This is characteristic of *Within a Budding Grove*, particularly Part Two, where his observational and analytic energies are frequently channelled towards the things and people of the world around him, rather than inwards to his own mind and memory, as at the start and end of *Swann's Way*. By contrast to the first volume of the novel, *Within a Budding Grove* is a largely linear narrative of discovery, albeit with proleptic signposts here and there pointing towards later volumes.

The opening to Part One offers insight into the subjectivity of perception, the nature of identity and the effects of the passage of time. In 'Combray', Swann was described as discreet about his social connections and well informed about art; now, to the Narrator's father's mind, he is 'a vulgar show-off', while Cottard, the awkward, unassured doctor of 'Swann in Love', is deemed an 'eminent' guest (*BG*, 1; *JF*, 347), now a professor, revered by colleagues and patients alike. The changes in both men illustrate that identity is fluid and shifting, or, to put it differently, that each of us has several identities that are manifest at different times and under different circumstances.

Norpois's role is double-edged: the old diplomat persuades the Narrator's sceptical father that a literary career is not necessarily a bad thing for his son yet he also deflates the would-be writer, first by remaining silent upon reading the Martinville vignette, then, at the mention of Bergotte, tearing into him, identifying his writings' 'bad influence' on the Narrator's piece, describing them as (amongst other things) 'flaccid' and 'altogether lacking in virility' (*BG*, 51–2; *JF*, 379). Norpois's remarks persuade the Narrator of his 'intellectual nullity' (*BG*, 53; *JF*, 380) and his father's capitulation makes him suddenly 'conscious of [himself] in Time' (*BG*, 63; *JF*, 386): he realizes that he is subject to the laws of Time and therefore already on the road towards old age and death which, with all hope of an artistic vocation now crushed, looks barren and unforgiving. For all that, he still delights in playing with Gilberte in the Champs-Élysées. This leads to a brief, erotic encounter, in which his physical pleasure culminates so suddenly that he laments, characteristically, that it took 'a form which I could not even pause for a moment to analyse' (*BG*, 76; *JF*, 395). Soon choking fits, much to his distress, prevent him from seeing Gilberte for an extended period, then one day an unexpected letter arrives from her, inviting him to tea. His love is redoubled and he starts to frequent the Swann residence, something previously possible only in the realm of his imagination.

As well as recounting his interactions with Gilberte, the Narrator also casts light on her mother's rapidly developing salon, so different from the '"official world"' to which her husband used to belong: 'like a kaleidoscope', the Narrator remarks, 'which is every now and then given a turn, society arranges successively in different orders elements which one would have supposed immutable, and composes a new pattern.' 'These new arrangements', he continues,

> are produced by what a philosopher would call a 'change of criterion.'
> The Dreyfus case brought about another, at a period rather later than
> that in which I began to go to Mme Swann's, and the kaleidoscope once
> more reversed its coloured lozenges. Everything Jewish, even the elegant
> lady herself, went down, and various obscure nationalists rose to take its
> place. If instead of the Dreyfus case there had come a war with Germany, the pattern of the kaleidoscope would have taken a turn in the
> other direction. (*BG*, 103; *JF*, 412)

This optical instrument is one of many incorporated into the *Search*, which is so concerned with perception, vision and insight. In referring to the Dreyfus case the Narrator anticipates one of the major themes of *The Guermantes Way* and the final, speculative sentence is a chilling prolepsis: a war with Germany did of course come, and its impact on society and individuals' prejudices is explored in *Time Regained*.

One day, *chez* Swann, the Narrator hears Odette play Vinteuil's sonata and the reflection this prompts, in effect a short essay on the reception and understanding of complex works of art, is a good example of the generic hybridity of Proust's novel. Here, as a little later when, upon meeting Bergotte, the Narrator offers a similar, sustained discussion of style in the novel, we find at work Proust's irrepressible urge to sound the depths of any experience, particularly aesthetic ones. Upon examination, such passages often reveal themselves to be reflexively instructive, offering insight into the act we carry out as we read the *Search*. 'Since I was able to enjoy everything that this sonata had to give me only in a succession of hearings', the Narrator confides, 'I never possessed it in its entirety: it was like life itself' ['elle ressemblait à la vie'] (*BG*, 119; *JF*, 423); or, one might suggest, like Proust's novel. At the key moment of exaltation before the trees at Hudimesnil, whose allure he cannot quite comprehend, a similar formulation is used: Mme de Villeparisis' carriage moves off, 'bearing me away from what alone I believed to be true, what would have made me truly happy; it [the carriage] was like my life' ['elle ressemblait à ma vie'] (*BG*, 345; *JF*, 569). The echo between these images highlights the underlying connections between the experiences being discussed: the beauties of art and of the natural world cannot be comprehensively known and, as time rushes on, carrying us relentlessly forward, we cannot comfortably apprehend and categorize all that we see and feel. These are the conditions that provoke the Narrator's frustration during his first trip to the theatre, where the words spoken on stage cannot be lingered over like those of a written text (*BG*, 23; *JF*, 361).

In 'Mme Swann at Home', as well as seeking knowledge of art and nature the Narrator must also come to terms with the vicissitudes of love. Gilberte eventually tires of him and when she chooses a dance lesson over his company he decides to effect an immediate separation, despite his love being unaltered, and his continued assiduity at Odette's salon. This section tracks the suffering felt in the absence of a loved one, as well as the painful self-scrutiny that any break-up inevitably provokes. The Narrator's turmoil recalls Swann's earlier in the novel and prepares the ground for his later relation with Albertine. When we are in love, he states, love cannot be contained within us:

> It radiates towards the loved one, finds there a surface which arrests it, forcing it to return to its starting-point, and it is this repercussion of our own feeling which we call the other's feelings and which charms us more then than on its outward journey because we do not recognise it as having originated in ourselves. (*BG*, 214; *JF*, 482–3)

This conception of love is constructed by the Narrator in the depths of his despair. It shatters the romantic conception of love as mutual admiration and understanding but, as Proust illustrates elsewhere in the novel, in love very often we see, hear and understand *what we want to*, and not what is apparent to disinterested onlookers.

When the Narrator meets Elstir, he learns a great deal about perspective and our habitual modes of perception. This does not teach him how to be happy in love but it gives the reader a greater sense of how, pessimistic as it may be, many aspects of the conception of love described above are in fact active in our daily existence. Getting to grips with Elstir's paintings requires a rethinking of what we take for granted in our field of vision; so doing offers a new version of the world, shows us that if we make the slightest adjustment in our apprehension of things they can appear to us comprehensively changed. 'We do not receive wisdom', Elstir remarks, 'we must discover it for ourselves, after a journey that no one else can take for us, which no one can spare us, for wisdom is the point of view from which we look at the world' (*BG*, 513, trans. mod.; *JF*, 678). Elstir's advice holds true well beyond the sphere of painting, and when the Narrator feels ready finally to embark upon his work in *Time Regained*, the tenor of his remarks in the Guermantes' library is in keeping with Elstir's words here.

Towards the close of 'Mme Swann at Home', the Narrator makes a sudden, spontaneous decision to see Gilberte again. On his way to her house, however, from his carriage he sees her out strolling with a young man. When he arrives *chez* Swann, pretending not to have seen Gilberte, he is told by Odette that she is out for a walk 'with one of her girl friends' (*BG*, 231; *JF*, 494). In his mind he and Gilberte were already reunited, as if they had never been apart, but, as so

often in the *Search*, this chance event has a far greater impact than any carefully planned encounter: by all appearances Gilberte has a new love and this
sends the Narrator crashing back into despair. Much later, in *Time Regained*,
Gilberte explains that she was walking with the actress, Léa, who was dressed
as a man. In the intervening volumes we see how much the Narrator suffers
through his fear of the great unknown that lesbian love represents for him;
although he does suffer as a result of what he sees, we might say in retrospect
that his ignorance of the identity of Gilberte's companion in fact prevented
him from the excessive turmoil such knowledge would doubtless have provoked. For all his desperation, his analysis of love is extremely lucid, often
focusing on the way time – that element over which we have no control – is
frequently the determining factor in our frustrations:

> time is the very thing that we are least willing to allow, for our suffering
> is acute and we are anxious to see it brought to an end. And then, too,
> the time which the other heart will need in order to change will have
> been spent by our own heart in changing itself too, so that when the
> goal we had set ourselves becomes attainable it will have ceased to be
> our goal. (*BG*, 237; JF, 497)

So try as we might to improve our outlook or our mental wellbeing, the Narrator
seems to be saying, even our best-intentioned efforts are futile. Suffering in
love is a painful business but as the comments above illustrate, with suffering, a 'journey from which no one can spare us', to use Elstir's words, comes
wisdom.

   Part One concludes with Odette and the attention she attracts as she walks
in the Avenue du Bois. The Narrator delights in the apparent symbiosis of the
seasons and her clothes, the beauty and elegance of her garments (whose traits
of style his older self finds sorely lacking in the women he sees on his return to
the Bois years later, the temporal perspective from which *Swann's Way* draws
to its close). In the warm spring air, Odette removes her jacket; the Narrator
folds it over his arm:

> I would see, and would lengthily gaze at … a lining of mauve satinette
> which, ordinarily concealed from every eye, was yet just as delicately
> fashioned as the outer parts, like those Gothic carvings on a cathedral,
> hidden on the inside of a balustrade eighty feet from the ground, as
> perfect as the bas-reliefs over the main porch, and yet never seen by any
> living man until, happening to pass that way upon his travels, an artist
> obtains leave to climb up there among them. (*BG*, 248; JF, 504–5)

The cathedral, Proust's structural paradigm par excellence, appears here growing in all its stony solidity from the unlikely source of a 'mauve satinette' lining.
Bringing together different forms of artisanship (as he did in *Swann's Way*,

comparing Françoise's efforts with cuts of beef to Michelangelo's labours with blocks of marble), Proust encourages readers to think on different levels at once, to consider the small scale and the soaring and to see what they share. When we encounter such images (and there are many) in the *Search*, and pause to trace their logic and interconnections, our actions are analogous to those of the Narrator and the artist in the image he creates. 'I should construct my book,' the Narrator remarks in the closing stages of the novel, 'I dare not say ambitiously like a cathedral, but quite simply like a dress' (*TR*, 432; 2390); the cathedral image just examined nuances this apparent modesty. Structural beauty in nature is also celebrated in *Within a Budding Grove*, when a 'gigantic fish' the Narrator is served is described as being constructed 'like a polychrome cathedral of the deep' (*BG*, 315–16; *JF*, 551).

'Place-names: The Place' begins with a bold chronological gear-change: we jump forward two years to a point when the Narrator, having 'arrived at a state of almost complete indifference to Gilberte' (*BG*, 253; *JF*, 511), travels to Balbec. In the place-name we hear the first syllable of *Alber*tine's name, whose life, thereafter, is ineradicably linked to his own. The trip is an important step in the Narrator's personal development as it is his first extended absence from his mother. He is accompanied, however, by Françoise and his grandmother, whose knocks on the partition wall between their rooms reassure him of her presence when he is alone and coming to terms with their new circumstances at the Grand Hotel. On the train approaching Balbec the Narrator has a highly instructive experience; as the sun rises, a pink colour fills the sky:

> It brightened; the sky turned to a glowing pink which I strove, glueing my eyes to the window, to see more clearly, for I felt that it was related somehow to the most intimate life of Nature, but, the course of the line altering, the train turned, the morning scene gave place in the frame of the window to a nocturnal village … beneath a firmament still spangled with all its stars, and I was lamenting the loss of my strip of pink sky when I caught sight of it anew, but red this time, in the opposite window which it left at a second bend in the line; so that I spent my time running from one window to the other to reassemble, to collect on a single canvas the intermittent, antipodean fragments of my fine, scarlet, ever-changing morning, and to obtain a comprehensive view and a continuous picture of it. (*BG*, 268; *JF*, 520–1)

This powerfully visual entry into Balbec announces the painterly preoccupations developed there. The scene memorably illustrates how we can experience time seemingly moving at different speeds at once. The train travels at one speed on a roughly horizontal axis while on a vertical axis, at a different speed, the rising sun performs its daily spectacle of turning darkness into light. Into this scene Proust introduces the movement of his ever-curious Narrator dashing back and forth, trying once again, quite literally, to 'see more clearly into the sources of his rapture'. One single, capacious sentence gathers this all in, just as the Narrator in that very sentence – and over the longer duration of the novel itself – seeks to piece together fragmentary impressions into a 'comprehensive' and 'continuous' view.

Raptures of this sort are balanced by disappointments of a kind with which we are now familiar: the Balbec church does not cling to a cliff, battered by squalls and sea spray as the Narrator had imagined, but, situated inland at Balbec-en-Terre, is found among the unpoetic surroundings of a savings bank and the omnibus office (*BG*, 274; *JF*, 524). Blinkered by this discovery (the shock of the real, we might say), he gazes with indifference on the statuary so long anticipated; it is not until Elstir explains its accomplishments ('it's the finest illustrated Bible that the people have ever had'; *BG*, 485; *JF*, 660) that the Narrator realizes what his preoccupations had prevented him from registering.

Balbec provides a microcosm of French society for the Narrator's analysis and exploration. At the head of the social hierarchy is Mme de Villeparisis, an old acquaintance of the Narrator's grandmother whom they meet unexpectedly. Her parents entertained Balzac, Hugo, Chopin and Liszt, amongst others, on which resolutely Sainte-Beuve-ian grounds she judges them as artists; her family are Guermantes who now become a step closer in accessibility for the Narrator. When he first encounters Robert de Saint-Loup, Mme de Villeparisis's nephew, who becomes his closest friend and ally, the description of him, like that of his uncle, Charlus, includes details of attitude, appearance and dress that point towards an ambiguous gender identity which develops throughout the remainder of the novel. When Charlus first appears, before his introduction to the Narrator, his gait and gestures lead the Narrator to take him for 'a hotel crook', 'a thief' and 'a lunatic' (*BG*, 383–4; *JF*, 594), terms of comparison which, by association, place the baron revealingly and unexpectedly from the outset in the company of some of the least desirable members of society.

When Bloch, holidaying at Balbec, reveals that one might do more than merely dream about the girls and young women they see, the Narrator's excited response ranges characteristically from the corporeal to the metaphysical to the cosmic: 'from the day on which I had first known that their cheeks could be kissed, I had become curious about their souls. And the universe had appeared to me more interesting' (*BG*, 336; *JF*, 564). The Narrator becomes absorbed in the actions of the little band of girls who roam the resort. A certain dynamism and vitality bind them together; they move differently and at a different pace to most of the sedentary holidaymakers. Proust's images for the girls, too many to enumerate here, are drawn from many domains, but the majority relate to the seaside and to nature, the environments in which the girls move. Accordingly we might note that Proust's images are often metonymic in nature, which is to say they are motivated by and drawn from the specific context in which they appear.

Part of the girls' initial allure derives from the Narrator's temporary inability to establish any demarcation between them. Out of 'the continuous transmutation of a fluid, collective and mobile beauty' (BG, 428; JF, 623), however, emerges Albertine, but she shares the group's polymorphousness: the Narrator struggles repeatedly to recall the position of her beauty spot when visualizing her after she has left him alone and, as their relation develops, his jealousy is continually spurred by the impossibility of his knowing, let alone controlling, her multiple selves.

The Narrator's knowledge of art and artistic method develops in parallel with his affections for the band of girls. He realizes, though, that his thoughts of them are often, in fact, thoughts of 'the mountainous blue undulations of the sea', concluding that 'the most exclusive love for a person is always a love for something else' (BG, 476–7; JF, 655). Soon afterwards, examining Elstir's paintings, he realizes that 'the charm of each of them lay in a sort of metamorphosis of the objects represented, analogous to what in poetry we call metaphor, and that, if God the Father had created things by naming them, it was by taking away their names or giving them other names that Elstir created them anew' (BG, 479; JF, 656). These examples suggest that an art like Elstir's, as exemplified in his painting of the Carquethuit harbour (BG, 480–1; JF, 657), is aesthetically successful because its method in fact mirrors the workings of the human heart, whose indirections we stand to understand better thanks to our contemplation of art.

Under Elstir's tutelage the Narrator's vision of the world around him gains greater depth. When he realizes that Elstir's portrait of a young woman dressed as a man, entitled *Miss Sacripant, Oct 1872*, depicts a youthful Odette, and subsequently that the wise painter of Balbec was therefore the vulgar 'Monsieur Biche' of 'Swann in Love', another perspective on the plurality of identity becomes apparent, which gradually colours the Narrator's developing familiarity with Albertine. He feels surprised by her use of language, which suggests 'a degree of civilisation and culture' he never imagined the 'bacchante with the bicycle, the orgiastic muse of the golf-course' to have before they became acquainted, a point that highlights the inevitable 'optical errors' of our first impressions (BG, 524; JF, 685). Albertine's facial expressions and the words she utters seem so complex a proposition that the Narrator metaphorically casts himself in the role of the schoolboy translator 'faced by the difficulties of a piece of Greek prose' (*BG*, 534; *JF*, 691). Albertine's lure of the unknown (in terms of language, appearance, background, tastes) is extremely powerful for the Narrator. Eventually she expresses her liking for him in a note that is neither equivocal nor gushing – 'Je vous aime bien', she writes [I do like you] (*BG*, 567, trans. mod.; *JF*, 715). With this, the Narrator's mind is set spinning and when Albertine, spending a night at the Grand Hotel in order to catch an early train next morning, asks him to spend the evening with her, he interprets this as an invitation to further intimacy. His assumption, however, is misplaced, and when his joy is at its peak ('Death might have struck me down', he remarks, 'and it would have seemed to me a trivial, or rather an impossible thing') he attempts to kiss Albertine, only for her, with a good measure of deflating humour, to evade his advances by pulling on the service bell 'with all her might' (*BG*, 593–4; *JF*, 729). This refusal is key in cementing the Narrator's love, which hitherto he had not thought to be founded on the desire for physical possession. Now apparent proof of Albertine's virtue makes her all the more desirable.

There is much that is alluring in the life that the Narrator tastes at Balbec but for all his discoveries, the closing note is one of disillusion, again – characteristically – relating to the passage of time. He came to Balbec expecting storm clouds and swathes of mist; the weather, in fact, has been uniformly fine, so as Françoise opens the curtains on the last of the summer sunshine, the scene thus revealed communicates not hope but a sense of stagnation for the Narrator. Albertine, however, like so many of the individuals we meet in the *Search*, is multiple and mobile; and her story has only just begun.

The Guermantes Way

Part One

The Narrator's family have moved to an apartment adjoining the Guermantes' Paris residence. Gradually the Narrator is disabused of the illusions he had woven around the name 'Guermantes' in his mind, but still he becomes fixated on the Duchesse. A trip to the Opéra to see Berma again offers an opportunity to reappraise her performance; Proust provides an extraordinary metaphorical account of the denizens of the faubourg Saint-Germain in their boxes, like water deities in enchanted grottoes. The Narrator seeks to gain access to the Duchesse through Saint-Loup, visiting him at his barracks at Doncières. Male companionship, class distinctions and military strategy are discussed at length. He returns to Paris to find his grandmother changed through illness.

Saint-Loup introduces him to his mistress, Rachel, who, unbeknownst to Robert, the Narrator has previously encountered in a brothel with Bloch. Saint-Loup's violent response to Rachel's flirting with a dancer suggests, in an echo of Swann's relation with Odette, that love is impossible without jealousy. The long account of a matinée *chez* Mme de Villeparisis follows: complex social dynamics are observed, there is much talk of Dreyfus; prejudices and rifts provide tension and humour in equal measure. Charlus offers to serve as a mentor for the Narrator but his motives are ambiguous. Part One closes with the Narrator's grandmother suffering a stroke.

Part Two

Chapter One details the grandmother's illness and death. In the much longer Chapter Two Saint-Loup breaks with Rachel; Albertine visits the Narrator; and a greatly anticipated amorous assignation with Mme de Stermaria falls through. He is finally invited to dinner by the Duchesse de Guermantes, an event narrated at exhaustive length. The same evening he visits Charlus who harangues him for neglecting to respond to his offer of guidance and allegedly speaking ill of him. Charlus rants, mocking the Narrator's ignorance of manners, aesthetics, society; he returns home quite bewildered. An invitation from the Princesse de Guermantes causes delight and disbelief. The volume ends with Swann announcing his terminal illness to the Duc and Duchesse, who unthinkingly fob him off, more concerned about the colour of the Duchesse's shoes than the ominous pallor about their old friend's cheeks.

The Guermantes Way, as Malcolm Bowie has neatly summarized, 'is the story of a youthful infatuation with superior people told by the scathing critic of human vanity that the youth concerned has now become'.[4] This combination of wide-eyed wonder and cutting critique brings insight, humour and irony. The social set-pieces are wrought in luxuriant yet purposeful prose, laced through with wit and studded with observations of the human animal that, for all their great length, make for extremely memorable reading.

A reflection on names – a familiar theme by now – begins the volume, picking up the Narrator's concerns with structure, duration and longevity. The Guermantes name can be traced back beyond the time of the construction of France's great cathedrals in the twelfth and thirteenth centuries (*G*, 6; 756); the family it represents thus by association has an enduring historicity and something, perhaps, of the four-dimensionality discerned in the Combray church. Readers should recall that before the war *The Guermantes Way* had been envisaged as the second of the *Search*'s three projected volumes. This might explain why surprisingly Françoise is described as already having 'snow-white hair' and being 'in her old age' (*G*, 10; 758–9). Her remarkable resilience, still being at the Narrator's side in *his* old age in *Time Regained*, would be less incongruous had *Sodom and Gomorrah* and the Albertine volumes not made us quite so aware of the many intervening years between the family's change of address in *The Guermantes Way* and the Narrator's revelations in the novel's final volume.

While much of *The Guermantes Way* is dedicated to the interactions of the aristocracy, through the conversations of Françoise and the Guermantes' domestic staff and the exposure we receive to the *demi-monde* to which Robert's mistress Rachel belongs, Proust's critical eye takes in a social panorama reaching well beyond the faubourg Saint-Germain. The threshold to this magical world, so long experienced by the Narrator only in his mind, takes material form in the Guermantes' rather shabby doormat (*G*, 26; 769). Undeterred by this unexpected reality, the Narrator is soon waiting outside each morning to catch a glimpse of Mme de Guermantes, as he did at the end of *Within a Budding Grove* for Mme Swann. And just as he realized that his love for Albertine was for a multitude of disparate figures who made up the girl of that name, so with Mme de Guermantes he realizes that he loves not any single one of her various manifestations, seen at different times and in different weathers, but rather 'the invisible person who set all this outward show in motion' (*G*, 65; 794). This suggests that his love is in fact for his *idea* or idealized construction of the woman and not the Duchesse herself.

He is able to come to this reasoned conclusion thanks, in part, to the lesson learned on his second trip to see Berma. He explains:

> We feel in one world, we think, we give names to things in another; between the two we can establish a certain correspondence, but not bridge the gap … The difference which exists between a person or a work of art that are markedly individual and the idea of beauty exists just as much between what they make us feel and the idea of love or of admiration. Wherefore we fail to recognise them. (*G*, 49; 784)

The Narrator acknowledges here the disjunction between sensation – our body's experience of the impressions made on us by the outside world – and the workings of the intellect that seeks to rationalize and categorize them. We encountered this tension in *Swann's Way* when the Narrator outlined the distinctions between voluntary and involuntary memory (*SW*, 50–5; 44–7); progressively we recognize that it is a driving force in much of the Narrator's speculative thinking.

When he makes a trip to the garrison town of Doncières to visit Saint-Loup, with remarkable attention to the experience of sound, he anatomizes the process of acquainting oneself with unfamiliar surroundings as he waits in Saint-Loup's room. Staying in the hotel in the town subsequently gives rise to an extended reflection on sleep, its strangeness, its different varieties (G, 89–96; 810–14); these pages recall and develop the musings of the 'Combray' overture, adding further nuance to the Narrator's always ongoing analysis of the nature of consciousness.

In the societal scenes later in the volume there is much emphasis on the vacuity of worldly interaction. At Doncières, however, when a companion suggests that in a military historian's narrative 'the most trivial happenings … are only the outward signs of an idea which has to be elucidated and which often conceals other ideas, like a palimpsest' (G, 119; 829), Saint-Loup reveals his intellect, holding forth with great verve on military history and strategy. The palimpsest, a manuscript that has been erased and over-written, but on which the earlier text can still be discerned, is a useful fig-ure to keep in mind, since repeatedly in the Search we encounter scenarios which seem to bear the marks of episodes we have already read. Indeed, after Saint-Loup's impromptu seminar, the Narrator describes how he suffers from not seeing Mme de Guermantes (G, 131; 837–8) in terms that recall the pages exploring the suffering he felt during his separation from Gilberte in the previous volume. This is not the final layer of the Proustian palimp-sest, however: The Fugitive details at length his extensive suffering following Albertine's disappearance.

He speaks with his grandmother by telephone for the first time from Doncières: technology isolates her voice from the visual support that usually accompanies it; as a result, rather than being comforted, the Narrator detects a sadness and fragility he had never previously discerned in her voice. His return to Paris painfully brings presence, absence and suffering into conjunc-tion: returning unannounced and entering the room where his grandmother sits is to be 'the spectator of [his] own absence' (G, 155; 853). He remarks that 'we never see the people who are dear to us save in … the perpetual motion of our incessant love for them, which, before allowing the images that their faces present to reach us, seizes them in its vortex and flings them back upon the idea that we have always had of them' (G, 156; 853). Until, that is, a chance event prevents our intelligence from deceiving us and we see reality for what it is. Revealed momentarily to the Narrator, then, 'sitting on the sofa … red-faced, heavy and vulgar, sick, daydreaming … [was] an overburdened old woman whom [he] did not know' (G, 157; 854). This episode illustrates how we protect ourselves from what we do not wish to confront – above all, death – and how chance occurrences can gain great significance in forcing us to face up to reality.

Before the Villeparisis matinée, the Narrator lunches and visits the theatre with Saint-Loup and Rachel. Relativism and point of view are seen again to be key in affairs of the heart: Saint-Loup first encountered Rachel performing on stage and he remains, in part, enraptured by this version of her. Like Swann with Odette (also a sometime actress: the palimpsest again), he lavishes vast sums of money on his mistress, a situation all the more pitiful for the reader, knowing (as Saint-Loup does not) that when the Narrator saw her in the brothel she could be anyone's for twenty francs. At the theatre Robert vents his frustration at his inability to control Rachel by slapping a journalist for failing to extinguish a cigar. Moments later in the street a man propositions Saint-Loup. The cascade of punches he unleashes on the man is defamiliarized in the Narrator's description, whose rendering of the rapid reconfigurations of forms in space is redolent of cubist and futurist visual art (*G*, 205–6; 885–6). Saint-Loup's violent reaction in the street recalls the story he himself told of Charlus's brutal response to a man who made similar overtures to him (see *BG*, 381; *JF*, 592–3). The parallel between Uncle and nephew, both of whom will be revealed, in due course, to be homosexual, is striking.

In Doncières and Paris, throughout the social spectrum, one topic is seldom far from people's lips: the Dreyfus Affair. Anti-Dreyfusism is the dominant position of the establishment and leading society figures; Saint-Loup's openly expressed *dreyfusard* convictions therefore sit uneasily with his military colleagues and relations alike. Odette, seeking acceptance by the social elite, perversely speaks out against Dreyfus despite her Jewish husband, and, according to the Narrator, having previously assured him of her conviction of Dreyfus's innocence (*G*, 302; 947): those climbing the social ladder must adjust their script according to their audience. Mme de Guermantes leaves as soon as she sees Odette arrive, such is her disinclination to make her acquaintance (*G*, 301–2; 947). For the Narrator, however, seeing Odette again is instructive since he has recently learnt from Charles Morel, the son of his great-uncle's valet, that Odette, besides being the androgynous 'Miss Sacripant', was also the 'lady in pink' who so enraptured him as a boy (see *G*, 304–5; 949–50). Illustrating the grip the Dreyfus case had on the nation, when the Narrator returns home, he finds his family's butler and the Guermantes' butler carrying on effectively the same conversation that Norpois and Bloch had had *chez* Villeparisis. As he puts it, the arguments 'contended on high among the intellectuals … were fast spreading downwards into the subsoil of popular opinion' (*G*, 340; 973). In society, however, as the Narrator's often biting commentary attests, what parades itself as knowledge, discernment and intelligence is frequently bluff, received opinion and crass ignorance.

As they are leaving, Charlus suggests to the Narrator that they walk together a while (*G*, 318; 958). He proposes that he might serve as mentor to the young man. Readers will have little doubt about the subtext here, but the Narrator, although a little confused, remains apparently unaware of Charlus's motivations, despite Mme de Villeparisis' unambiguously expressed disapproval of his consorting with Charlus away from her salon (*G*, 325–6; 963).

At home, his grandmother's health has deteriorated but the fictional Dr du Boulbon, said to be a protégé of Charcot (1825–93), the founder of modern neurology, recognizes the patient's literary spirit and determines through talking to her that her complaint is as much nervous as it is physiological (*G*, 346–7; 977–8). As we read the doctor's encouraging words ('Submit to being called a neurotic … Everything we think of as great has come to us from neurotics'), even a superficial knowledge of Proust's own health suggests that this apologia for neurosis is not wholly disinterested: 'we enjoy fine music, beautiful pictures', continues Boulbon, 'but we do not know what they cost those who wrought them in insomnia, tears, spasmodic laughter, urticaria, asthma, epilepsy, a terror of death which is worse than any of these' (*G*, 350; 979). Mind and body cannot be decoupled: the sublime aesthetic products of intelligence, such as Proust's book, come at a cost to their creators measurable in the all-too-human terms of suffering and pain.

Boulbon's recommendation of fresh air and walks is followed, only for the Narrator's grandmother to suffer a stroke when accompanying him to the Champs-Élysées. Proust is notorious for his long sentences, but the start of Part Two offers a fine example (and there are a great many in the *Search*) of his under-acknowledged mastery of impact through *brevitas*: 'She was not yet dead. But I was already alone.' These stark lines (*G*, 359; 989) intimate once more the Narrator's awareness of how the brain often works at speeds quite distinct from those of the phenomena to which it responds.

Interwoven in Part Two's opening chapter are two intriguing character studies: Bergotte, gravely ill, is nevertheless an assiduous and unassuming visitor during the grandmother's final illness (*G*, 373–5; 998–9); the Duc de Guermantes, by contrast, appears just once, but his attentiveness to social formalities renders him chronically desensitized to the emotional drama on which he intrudes (*G*, 387–9; 1007–9). His blundering anticipates the obtuseness with which, in due course, he and the Duchesse greet Swann's news of his terminal illness. Bergotte's visits permit the Narrator a digression on the nature of artistic creation, which illustrates his developing sensibilities. Original artists proceed, he remarks, like oculists performing a treatment: when their work is done, we are asked to look on the world, which 'appears to us entirely different from the old world, but perfectly clear'. And this because the world 'is not created once and for all, but as often as an original artist comes along' (*G*, 376, trans. mod.; 1000). When the grandmother dies, the event is described in terms of an artistic process that connects several of the novel's key thematic threads: 'On that funerary bed, death, like a sculptor of the Middle Ages, had laid her down in the form of a young girl' (*G*, 397, trans. mod.; 1014).

After this tender closure on the permanence of death, Chapter Two opens with that most transient but emotive of things: a change in the weather, which 'is sufficient to create the world and ourselves anew' (*G*, 398; 1014). The Narrator, in bed, pieces together the world beyond his windows through his apprehensions of sound and colour, and reviews the memories roused by his observations. Saint-Loup, succumbing to family pressure, has split with Rachel and is posted to Morocco; he writes that in Tangier he has met Mme de Stermaria, a young woman in whom the Narrator had expressed an interest at Balbec, now a divorcee and willing to dine with him (*G*, 400–1; 1015–16). This prospect sets his mind whirring in anticipation of amorous possibilities, whereupon Françoise unexpectedly announces Albertine, who enters, resembling 'an enchantress offering … a mirror that reflected time' (*G*, 404; 1018). She seems to embody all that enraptured the Narrator about their spell by the sea, yet at the same time she has matured in appearance, become yet more confident in her language, her movements. Just as the Combray landscape sprang forth from the Narrator's teacup, now he feels that preserved in Albertine are all his impressions of a cherished series of seascapes; 'in kissing her cheeks', he suggests 'I should be kissing the whole of Balbec beach' (*G*, 418; 1027).

When the kiss does occur, however, any romance there might have been dies in the detail of the description. But this is no surprise: beforehand he remarks that 'the knowledge that to kiss Albertine's cheeks was … possible … was a pleasure perhaps greater even than that of kissing them' (*G*, 417; 1026), and, sure enough, the stimulus offered by the consideration of his various desires and their potential outcomes is greater than that offered by the rather paltry physical act itself. All the while, however, part of the Narrator's mind remains preoccupied by the possible delights in store with Mme de Stermaria, but these are never tasted: she cries off at the last minute, and the pleasurable, tantalising 'what ifs' of anticipation become the despairing 'if onlys' of regret.

Between Albertine's kiss and Mme de Stermaria's no-show there glimmers a rare moment of hope becoming reality: Mme de Guermantes invites the Narrator to dinner, something akin to 'making acquaintance with a dream' (*G*, 433; 1037). After a series of vivid memories he has shortly before the day of the dinner, he remarks proleptically that had he remained alone, the enthusiasm he was experiencing 'might have borne fruit' and saved him 'the detour of many wasted years through which [he] was yet to pass before the invisible vocation of which this book is the history declared itself' (*G*, 459; 1053). Even before dining with the Guermantes he recognizes that time spent in society is 'temps perdu' – time lost or wasted – for the artist, who requires solitude to achieve his or her goals. Nevertheless, youthful curiosity prevails and he presses onwards to his first dinner *chez* Guermantes.

As he ponders their collection of Elstirs, further memories of Balbec emerge, alongside another reflection on perspective and artistic creation (*G*, 483–7; 1069–72). And just as perspective has its laws, so does society. The Duc rushes to introduce the Narrator to the Princesse de Parme not motivated by graciousness but because form dictates that 'the presence ... of anyone not personally known to a royal personage is an intolerable state of things'. Gradually the Narrator realizes the paradoxical effect of this slavery to etiquette: in society 'it is the surface that becomes essential and profound' (*G*, 492; 1074). Social players are expected to provide the right lines, respond to the right cues. Mme de Guermantes' witticisms are legendary and her quip about Charlus, an inveterate tease ('*taquin*' in French), being 'Taquin le superbe' (a pun on the Roman King 'Tarquinius Superbus', beautifully transmuted in English as 'Teaser Augustus'; *G*, 537; 1104) is such a hit that 'it would be served up again cold the next day at lunch ... and would reappear under various sauces throughout the week' (*G*, 538; 1104). Puns and facile anecdotes circulate in the salons, discussed with no less fervour than matters of politics and art, yet most *mondains* set little store by personal judgement, instead proffering conditioned responses which will gain the approval of those listening.

The Narrator comments on being mistaken for someone else, reflects on the 'numberless mistakes ... which accompany one's name in the file which society compiles about one' (*G*, 575, trans. mod.; 1128), and arrives at the conclusion, anticipating by several decades Jean-Paul Sartre's concept of 'being-for-others', that we are powerless to control the conception of ourselves constructed by those around us. The Narrator, seeking fulfilment beyond the stultifying vanities of society, strikingly describes his time there as 'les heures mondaines où j'habitais mon épiderme' [those hours in which I lived on the surface] (*G*, 610; 1150), his deeper self quite dormant. After long imagining such parties, firsthand experience underlines merely their 'barren frivolity' (*G*, 636; 1167).

With a mixture of exhilaration and melancholy he makes his way to his appointment with Charlus, described earlier by Mme de Guermantes, in keeping with the ambiguities of his identity thus far revealed, as being 'kind and sweet, [with] a delicacy, a warmth of heart that you don't find as a rule in men' (*G*, 587; 1135). These traits are scarcely evident, however, as Charlus, with almost uncontrolled emotion, launches a raging verbal assault on the Narrator. His pride is hurt (the Narrator did not write and may have spoken inappropriately of him) but he will not admit it: 'Do you imagine', he asks 'that the envenomed spittle of five hundred little gentlemen of your type … would succeed in slobbering so much as the tips of my august toes?' (*G*, 646; 1173). Charlus's eloquent fury is a joy to read; it draws us closer to his insecurities, further exhibits his erudition, exposes how his character is shaped by his class. Ultimately his rage subsides but he states that their relations are 'cut short … for all time' (*G*, 651; 1177), leaving the bemused Narrator to puzzle out why the baron should have prized so highly his reciprocated affections.

The nature of Charlus's designs becomes retrospectively clearer in the opening section of *Sodom and Gomorrah*, but for the remainder of *The Guermantes Way* intrigues of gender and desire are placed on hold as a few final layers are peeled from the social onion. When the Narrator receives an invitation from the Princesse de Guermantes his insecurities lead him to doubt its authenticity. Fearful of the ignominy of gatecrashing a society soirée he seeks confirmation from the Duc and Duchesse. Gazing over the courtyard, awaiting their return, the Narrator's thoughts turn to artistic matters. He ponders the multiplicity of the vista, recalling Venetian skylines and Dutch townscapes of paintings he has admired. These references are not contingent: they prepare the reader for Bergotte's death scene and the Venetian section of *The Fugitive*; they also underscore how solitude is necessary for the engagement of the Narrator's artistic vision. The Duc and Duchesse appear but have to prepare themselves for a series of evening engagements. Swann arrives, bringing the Duchesse outsized photographs of some rare coins he has recently discovered. The Narrator steals a moment to talk to Swann about the Affair; this permits Proust to remind readers of the positions of various prominent figures, positions which, as *Sodom and Gomorrah* shows, are far from definitively fixed.

The humour of the scene (for example, the Duc's stating that he is happy for the photographs to go in the Duchesse's room where he will not see them, 'oblivious of the revelation he was thus blindly making of the negative character of his conjugal relations'; *G*, 686; 1200) is tempered by the pathos of Swann's announcement of his illness. This refocuses attention on the theme of mortality, latent since the grandmother's death, now painfully present in the blundering Duc's choice of idioms ('she'll reach the dinner-table quite dead … I'm dying of hunger'; *G*, 690; 1203). Proust exhibits here his extraordinary ability to expose human foibles whilst balancing pain with laughter. Mme de Guermantes 'could find nothing in the code of conventions' indicating the right course of action between 'two duties as incompatible as getting into a carriage to go out to dinner and showing compassion for a man who was about to die', and so, tellingly, she thinks 'that the best way of settling the conflict would be to deny that any existed' (*G*, 688; 1202). This ostrich-like response neatly encapsulates the vision of high society that emerges from *The Guermantes Way*. It is not a snobbish celebration of the old aristocracy; the Narrator may at times be entranced by them, but he also offers an uncompromising critique of the blinkered self-centredness that contributed in large measure to their demise.

Sodom and Gomorrah

Part One

A voyeuristic scene reminiscent of that involving Mlle Vinteuil at Montjouvain in 'Combray' opens the volume: the Narrator observes Charlus and Jupien meeting by chance in the Guermantes' courtyard. After watching Charlus's initial overtures, he eavesdrops on them having sex in Jupien's workshop. Thus enlightened, extrapolating from this episode, the Narrator subsequently discusses the plight of the 'descendants of Sodom', describing the various types of 'invert'.

Part Two

Chapter One begins with an extensive account of the Princesse de Guermantes' reception: Dreyfus is much discussed, as are various individuals' shifts in allegiance. The Narrator receives a late-night visit from Albertine: his behaviour anticipates his later, neurotic possessiveness. Returning to Balbec he experiences the delayed realization that his grandmother is dead. In Chapter Two happiness with Albertine seems possible but is tinged with suspicions, as when Cottard remarks on how she dances with Andrée. Various developments fuel the Narrator's anxieties: Bloch's sister's relation with an actress; M. Nissim Bernard's proclivities; Charlus's first meeting with Charlie Morel, son of Uncle Adolphe's valet. A long sequence narrates an evening party at 'La Raspelière', the residence rented by the Verdurins. Much humour derives from the uneasy interaction between the bourgeois Verdurin 'faithful' and their social superiors: the Cambremers, owners of 'La Raspelière', and Charlus, accompanying his new love, Morel. Chapter Three brings revelations of Morel's vices and further anxiety about Albertine's true nature. After a tiff Charlus informs Morel he will fight a duel, a lie calculated to bring his lover back. And so the relations stumble on from deception to reconciliation, with little sense of enduring happiness or freedom. Loosely connected vignettes relate seaside life and the convivial train journeys of the Verdurin faithful. Tired of her company and strained by his suspicions, the Narrator decides that marrying Albertine would be madness. In the brief Chapter Four, however, he unexpectedly discovers her long-term acquaintance with Mlle Vinteuil and her friend. This 'proof' of Albertine's lesbianism shatters his decision to break with her. Only suffering remains for him, yet he resolves to return to Paris with her, somehow to keep her from her vice; he informs his mother he must marry Albertine.

Part One provides a study in Proust's remarkable manipulation of context and metaphor. Waiting, overlooking the Guermantes' courtyard, the Narrator reflects on the chance events that must occur in order for certain flowers to be fertilized. He has his eyes on a particular plant and, eventually, a bee does enter his field of vision, but it is soon clear that the tropes relating the vagaries of plant fertilization have a more complex purpose than the illustration of his taste for amateur botany. The Narrator studies Charlus and Jupien in the way a botanist might scrutinize sub-varieties of plants. His initial discovery, afforded by perceiving the baron at ease, thinking himself unobserved, is that he resembles a woman. He then watches this previously unseen version of Charlus approaching Jupien, who 'struck poses with the coquetry that the orchid might have adopted on the providential arrival of the bee' (*SG*, 5; 1212). Each man recognizes the other's nature and capitalizes on the opportunity offered him by circumstance. The penny drops: 'everything that hitherto had seemed to my mind incoherent, became intelligible, appeared self-evident' (*SG*, 16–17; 1219). Contemporary attitudes classed homosexuality as a 'vice', 'a curse', 'an incurable disease' (*SG*, 17–18; 1219–20); Proust draws parallels with similar attitudes to Jews at the time, but suggests lyrically that homosexuality, like the vast, proliferating sentence that communicates the point, reaches far and wide, is dispersed through every stratum of society. Charlus is identified as one for whom 'the satisfaction … of [his] sexual needs depends upon the coincidence of too many conditions, and of conditions too difficult to meet' (*SG*, 32; 1229). Yet he and Jupien surmount the barriers to their pleasure, a succession of events 'almost of the same order and no less marvellous' than the fecundation of the orchid by the bee. Contrary to society's dominant views, to the observing Narrator 'everything about it seemed to me imbued with beauty' (*SG*, 33, trans. mod.; 1229). Lesbian relations are not treated until much later; when they are, the Narrator's perspective is quite different: they represent a '*terra incognita*' for the heterosexual male, a profound threat like a rival with 'different weapons' (*SG*, 597, 603; 1593, 1597).

As Charlus and Jupien's relation makes clear, desire pays little heed to social status; this phenomenon is repeatedly highlighted by Proust, often to comic ends, as evinced by the anecdote relating the Duc de Châtellerault's encounters with the usher who 'barks' out guests' names upon their arrival at the Princesse de Guermantes' residence (*SG*, 39–40, 42–3; 1235–6, 1237–8). The Narrator, much to his relief, is not *persona non grata* at the reception. Desperately trawling his memory for the name of a woman who starts speaking to him leads to an illuminating aside. Flawed memory is key to our appreciating the wonders of recollection, he suggests: 'infirmity alone makes us take notice and learn, and enables us to analyse mechanisms of which otherwise we should know nothing' (*SG*, 60; 1248); these comments might offer us some solace when our memories struggle with the sheer volume of Proust's novel.

Before seeing him unguarded in the Guermantes' courtyard, the Narrator had taken Charlus's emphasis on virility and his loathing of effeminacy at face value; at the Princesse's reception, however, alert now to the role-play that concealing secret identities obliges individuals to undertake, he dismantles false façades, attuned to the different levels of communication that can coexist on the social stage. Progressively he develops his ability to decipher the sign systems of the world in which he moves, which extend well beyond the domain of love and desire.

The guests' conversations and interactions are revealing on many levels: Vaugoubert, the old ambassador, is a homosexual whose professional obligations have almost wholly blunted his ability to recognize those of his own kind. He and Charlus are intriguing cases of how circumstance and environment can lead to divergent developments in what may have been initially similar characters. The Duc de Guermantes, who spoke jovially with Swann at the close of *The Guermantes Way*, now, just a few hours later in the real time of the narrative, derides Swann's *dreyfusard* position as one of 'ingratitude' towards the faubourg Saint-Germain which had for so long welcomed him as an equal (*SG*, 90; 1268). Swann is present but has been whisked off to the bottom of the garden where, rumour has it, the Prince is berating him for his Dreyfusism. In reality the Prince is taking the opportunity to tell his old friend that he *shares* his convictions, as does his wife (although they had each kept their thinking hidden for some time, fearing each other's disapproval; *SG*, 120–31; 1288–95). The kaleidoscope, then, is turning.

Interwoven with the socio-political chatter are the often unspoken currents of desire. Charlus's concentration on the face of the young Comte de Surgis is so profound as to make it resemble 'some rebus, some riddle, some algebraic problem, of which he must try to penetrate the mystery' (*SG*, 103; 1277). Saint-Loup sews seeds of amorous promise for the Narrator, speaking of the 'stunning women' one might find in 'maisons de passe' (houses of assignation, or brothels), citing as examples the aristocratic 'Mademoiselle … d'Orgeville' and 'in a different class of goods … Mme Putbus's chambermaid' (*SG*, 108–9; 1280), both of whom become long-term fixations for the Narrator, although neither is ever met. The Narrator thinks he meets Mlle d'Orgeville in *The Fugitive*, only to be victim to one of the novel's many cases of mistaken identity (*F*, 643–8; *AD*, 2027–31); later on, seeing the name of Mme Putbus in a hotel register is almost enough to keep him in Venice when he is due to leave (*F*, 748; *AD*, 2096).

The anecdotes and observations of *Sodom and Gomorrah* have much to teach us about desire, how it blinds us, the cruelties into which it pushes us, the insecurities and fears it instills in our minds, regardless of our sexual preferences. Charlus is said to have let a queen die 'rather than miss an appointment with the hair-dresser who was to singe his hair for the benefit of a bus-conductor whom he found prodigiously intimidating' (*SG*, 134; 1297). And the Narrator himself, returning home with the Duc and Duchesse, illustrates the rapid alterations of which desire is disarmingly capable. So close together are he and the Duchesse in the carriage (a proximity he had long only imagined) that she jokes about her accidentally treading on his feet being taken the wrong way, yet this leaves him unmoved for his mind is focused on Mlle d'Orgeville and Mme Putbus's chambermaid (*SG*, 142–3; 1302). As a result the Duchesse, even in toe-trampling proximity, is no longer bewitching; but when she speaks slightingly of Mme Putbus, the Narrator's devotion to these unknown figures suddenly dissolves. Mme de Guermantes invites him to the Princesse de Parme's costume ball, an event he would hitherto have leapt at the opportunity to attend, yet he declines, for the compass of his yearnings has shifted once more: 'I was interested not in the ball but in my rendezvous with Albertine' (*SG*, 144; 1303). Increasingly, from this moment on, Albertine is the primary object of the Narrator's attentions.

He awaits her midnight visit, providing a beautiful assessment of our emotional investment in the process of waiting for people we care about (*SG*, 149–51; 1307–8), before revealing how manipulative he can be in the service of his own satisfaction: spurred by jealousy and suspicion, he persuades Albertine to change her mind when she telephones to inform him she is not coming. Not to have her presence would be to rekindle the horrors of his bedtime trauma in Combray: Albertine's kiss is troublingly compared to his mother's, and now as then we realize the uncompromising tensions of the Narrator's psyche: 'the prospect of having to forgo a simple physical pleasure caused me an intense mental suffering' (*SG*, 149; 1306). Suffering is a keynote of *Sodom and Gomorrah*, a term that is never far away in the Narrator's analyses of love and desire. He arrives at the feeling that with regard to Albertine, 'out of that tangled mass of details of fact and falsehood, I should never unravel the truth: and that it would always be so, unless I were to imprison her (but prisoners escape) until the end' (*SG*, 154, trans. mod.; 1310). Before the shared life with Albertine that this statement adumbrates really begins, however, another form of suffering is experienced: 'the intermittencies of the heart.'

The Narrator travels to Balbec. The section opens in ludic mode with the hotel director's comically flawed French, but soon the tone changes: fatigued, stooping to take off his boots, the Narrator experiences the 'upheaval of [his] entire being' (*SG*, 179; 1326), a rush of emotion that suddenly recaptures the instant when his grandmother had helped him in a similar moment of physical weakness on their first trip to Balbec (*BG*, 284; *JF*, 531). Now, more than a year after her burial, 'because of the anachronism which so often prevents the calendar of facts from corresponding to the calendar of feelings', he finally 'became conscious that she was dead' (*SG*, 180; 1327). The intermittencies of the heart are negatively inflected involuntary memories that bring not a sense of recuperation but of loss. He feels temporarily reinstalled in the adolescent self that, fearful of his new surroundings, arrived at Balbec years before, but the sorrow from which he sought solace in his grandmother's arms is now that of mourning, which he must come to terms with alone. He tortures himself about being cruel to his grandmother when she arranged for a photograph to be taken (Françoise reveals to the Narrator – who is devastated – that his grandmother's apparent coquetry when the photograph was taken was born of a desire to conceal her grave illness and to leave him an image by which he might remember her; *SG*, 203; 1342); and as he attempts to take stock of an existence without her, at every turn he sees his mother, an eerie embodiment of the grandmother, carrying her handbag, reading her books and wearing her dressing gown. Such accoutrements are not necessary for the similarities to be painfully apparent, however, since, in the Narrator's memorable formulation, 'the dead annex the living who become their replicas and successors, the continuators of their interrupted life' (*SG*, 195; 1337).

During the Narrator's stay at Balbec we encounter several sparkling examples of Proust's ear for sociolects and idiolects: the lift-boy's crudeness and mistakes, the director's gaffes, Mme de Cambremer's *diminuendo* adjectives and the Guermantes' jargon, all of which add richness to this truly polyphonic novel. It is Albertine's words, however, and her actions that receive the keenest scrutiny. Her company, in the second chapter of Part Two, slowly appeases the intermittencies of the Narrator's heart and reignites his desire for happiness.

One afternoon a broken-down tram results in the Narrator bumping into Cottard at Incarville. In the casino, where they pass the time, a scene unfolds that profoundly alters the Narrator's perception of Albertine. She and her friends are there; Albertine is waltzing with Andrée. The Narrator comments to Cottard how well they dance, whereupon the doctor, ignoring that the Narrator knows the girls, remarks that 'they are certainly keenly roused. It's not sufficiently known that women derive most excitement through their breasts. And theirs, as you see, are touching completely' (*SG*, 225; 1356). Once more, a contingent event throws the Narrator into a spin: a man of science identifies in Albertine evidence of the vice he most fears, and hereafter almost every girl he sees becomes his rival.

Subsequently the Narrator's suspicions grow about Albertine's avowals of interest or apathy towards this or that outing or activity. After one exchange of leading questions and evasive answers, he concludes that ultimately he 'had no desire … to enter upon the terrible path of investigation, of multiform, unending vigilance' (*SG*, 231; 1360). The irony of this statement is extremely bitter, for this is just what he does: *The Captive* is the narrative of his journey down precisely that path. Moreover, already at this stage he lies, claiming, for instance, that he has long loved Andrée and not Albertine, in order to talk her round to a reconciliatory intimacy he did not have the confidence to seek without the safety net of artfully woven lies. His actions are based upon deep insecurities about whether anyone could actually love him. As ever, he has mental agility in surfeit, but common sense in short supply; he summarizes his position as that of 'those … whose self-analysis outweighs their self-esteem' (*SG*, 264; 1381). Characteristically, he pays scant acknowledgement to the pain his actions might inflict on Albertine. Indeed, sympathize periodically with him as we might, admiring his turns of phrase and his nimble mind, just as often in *Sodom and Gomorrah* and *The Captive* we see quite how self-centred, hypocritical and inconsistent he can be. He has no qualms about fantasizing about Mme Putbus's maid, for example, but when he remembers that Saint-Loup mentioned her possible taste for women, he trembles, fearful that she might find Albertine at Balbec and 'corrupt her' (*SG*, 277; 1390).

Balancing the tensions of jealousy and suspicion, the social scenarios of *Sodom and Gomorrah* are studded with portraiture and anecdotes which send up human vanities, illuminate desire's sway over the individual and repeatedly reveal how, despite the great diversity of humankind, in the grips of passion we very often have much in common. The figure of Mme de Cambremer, 'toothless', frothing at the mouth at the mere thought of Chopin (*SG*, 239; 1366) is hard to forget; similarly it is difficult to read without smirking the anecdote of the short-sighted M. Nissim Bernard propositioning the wrong rosy-faced twin and receiving a beating that puts him off tomatoes for life (*SG*, 291–3; 1400–1). Proust's text persistently switches between high and low, drawing a vast array of human experience into its purview.

Charlus, resembling the dandified old man feigning youth with cosmetics in Thomas Mann's *Death in Venice* (1912), meets Morel at Doncières station, a chance encounter reminiscent of that with Jupien at the start of the volume. The relationship between the aristocrat and the valet's son is nurtured then torn apart by the Verdurins. Just as the Prince and the Duc de Guermantes changed their allegiance during the Affair, so now Mme Verdurin is 'a sincere Dreyfusard' (*SG*, 327; 1423), she whose 'latent bourgeois anti-Semitism' had, we were told in *The Guermantes Way*, 'grown to a positive fury' (*G*, 288; 939). The Verdurins are just as capable of insensitivity and cruelty as their titled counterparts: '"It's dreadful"', M. Verdurin responds 'cheerfully' to the news of the death of their faithful pianist Dechambre and reports that his 'morbidly sensitive' wife 'almost wept' when she heard the news (*SG*, 344; 1434). Saniette is remorselessly mocked for sport, with no concern for the effects on his psyche. Their world is bizarrely binaristic: the fawning faithful are 'intelligent'; those who do not or will not come, or whose fidelity lapses, are 'boring' or 'stupid', although just a glance at the frequent occurrences of these terms shows how their conventional meanings have been all but entirely evacuated. The Cambremers tolerate their tenants since the rent provides for the upkeep of their residence at Féterne; their gardener's attitude, however, depicts in miniature the true relations across the class divide: '[he] groaned beneath the Verdurins' yoke, as though the place were … occupied by an invading army of roughneck soldiery' (*SG*, 365; 1447).

Charlus's presence among the Verdurin clan provokes some fascinating tensions relating to class and to sexuality. His 'morals' are generally overlooked and certainly not discussed in high society; *chez* Verdurin, however, he is less discreet and more notorious. M. Verdurin, seeking to dissimulate his ignorance regarding social protocol, remarks to Charlus that 'from the first words we exchanged, I realised that you were *one of us*! … you are *one of us*, it's as clear as daylight' (*SG*, 393; 1464). The construction 'en être' (translated in italics) is used to refer to homosexuality throughout the *Search*; Charlus accordingly fears what his blundering host is about to blurt out. Fortunately (laughably), Verdurin is referring to social belonging. Charlus, bristling, corrects the error that he is 'only a baron', reeling off his remarkable string of titles, concluding with a characteristically dismissive 'however, it's not of the slightest importance' (*SG*, 395; 1465).

As the evening draws to its end, Mme Verdurin tries to dissuade the Narrator from accepting a dinner invitation from the Cambremers ('the place is infested with bores'); in his fudged response he claims to 'have a young cousin [he] can't leave by herself' as a means of excusing his spending time with Albertine (*SG*, 425; 1484–5), thus contributing his own measure of obfuscation to the swirl of half-truths and lies circulating amongst the faithful. This evening with the Verdurins is the only one narrated in full, but it represents, metonymically we might say, many other such events. This technique of narrating once what was a repeated or customary event has been called 'iterative narrative' by Gérard Genette in his important essay 'Discours du récit' [Narrative Discourse]. These hours spent in bourgeois society are no more profitable in artistic terms than those spent *chez* Guermantes. When M. Verdurin comments that the weather seems to have changed as the Narrator prepares to leave, the effect is profound: 'these words filled me with joy, as though the dormant life, the resurgence of different combinations which they implied in nature, heralded other changes, occurring in my own life, and created fresh possibilities in it' (*SG*, 433; 1489). The sudden sentiment of joy here comes from a change in the weather ('le temps') but also from stepping outside the social bubble into a new relation with *time*: simply by opening the front door, 'on sentait qu'un autre "temps" occupait depuis un instant la scène' ('one felt that another time/weather had just taken possession of the scene': Proust's inverted commas around 'temps' draw attention to the polysemous value that cannot quite be captured in translation).

Given that dreams can have the clarity of consciousness, 'might consciousness have the unreality of a dream?' So ponders the Narrator at the start of Chapter Three (*SG*, 445; 1497). The mind's activity during sleep offers evidence of powerful creative potential the artist must harness in his or her work. The Narrator, however, spends much of his time fearfully testing the potential 'unreality' of whatever presents itself to him in his waking hours rather than channelling his creative capacities into a work of art.

Travelling alone while Albertine paints near Balbec, he recognizes that the feelings he has for her he previously felt for Mme de Stermaria and Mme de Guermantes: 'it was my fate to pursue only phantoms, creatures whose reality existed to a great extent in my imagination.' He looks around, feels that the trees by the road give him 'a silent counsel to set myself to work at last, before the hour of eternal rest had yet struck' (*SG*, 476; 1517). He cannot follow this counsel, however: Albertine's spell is too strong. He looks at her, at the face which tantalizes him with the 'enigma of her intentions'; she is 'a whole state of soul, a whole future existence that had assumed before my eyes the allegorical and fateful form of a girl' (*SG*, 485; 1523). The successful deciphering of this complex symbol will determine the future course of his life.

As their complex relationship unfolds, so alongside it does that of Charlus and Morel, separated by age and class, but bound together by desire, although not necessarily always of a mutual, erotic sort. Charlus, besotted, treats Morel like a ward or protégé, showering him with gifts and proffering advice ranging from the interpretation of Beethoven to the finer distinctions between varieties of pear (*SG*, 472–4; 1515–16). Morel, on the other hand, always puts himself first and happily deceives others for his own gain. Despite this he feels persecuted and rails against 'universal treachery'; in short he is 'a mass of contradictions' and, like the novel in which he appears, 'extraordinarily composite'

(*SG*, 498–9; 1532). The image used by the Narrator to describe Charlus's vulnerability as gradually he becomes an object of derision is full of pathos: he is like a fish unaware of the limits of its aquarium, the spectators beyond the glass and the presence of 'the all-powerful keeper who, at the unforeseen and fatal moment … will extract it without compunction' (*SG*, 518; 1544). His various travails that stud the chapter (the fictitious duel; his spying at the Maineville brothel, nearly – unwittingly – discovering Morel with the Prince de Guermantes; Morel's laughable stories of algebra lessons that 'soothe his nerves' until after 2 a.m.) almost make the Narrator's relation with Albertine look conventional. The chapter comes to its close, however, with a steady sense of routine, time and space measured out along the stations of the local railway line, their place-names now demystified by Brichot's etymologies.

In Chapter Four, this calm is shattered by Albertine's disclosure of her intimacy with Mlle Vinteuil and her friend (*SG*, 596; 1592). The past is not inert, neatly stored away: the memory of Montjouvain rushes painfully back to the Narrator, with Albertine transposed into the scene. His imagination works overtime, leaping from assumption to assumption; in self-preservation mode he adopts the habit he so fears in Albertine: lying. He veils his true emotions in a fabrication about being engaged to a woman, separating from her and fearing that he might commit suicide out of remorse. This keeps Albertine from guessing the reasons for his distress, but gazing at her he realizes that for him all is lost: the words she spoke magically embed her in the 'depths of [his] lacerated heart' before closing it up again, leaving him no idea of how to rid himself of this new suffering at the core of his being (*SG*, 612; 1602). Keeping her by his side may help limit further damage. Doing so will displease his mother, lukewarm at best about their relationship, but this regret is outweighed by a pathological fear of living without Albertine. So, with a fragile and part-feigned assurance that makes us squirm in our chairs, he announces his desire to marry her.

The Captive

The Captive details the Narrator's cohabitation with Albertine in Paris. His parents are absent with work and family commitments, leaving the couple alone with Françoise. The Narrator repeatedly states that he no longer loves Albertine yet his jealousy binds him to her. One day he almost catches her and Andrée *in flagrante*; the suspicions roused on this and similar occasions torment him. He finds some peace observing Albertine sleeping: unconscious, her ever-dispersed identities and unknowable desires are reeled in; only then does he feel that he possesses this 'fugitive being'. Gradually he recognizes the futility of trying to control her: contingent events, ill-formed cover stories and half-truths told to conceal earlier lies reveal more to him than years of dedicated investigation ever could. There are many extremely beautiful reflective passages: on changes in the weather, on the cries of street vendors, on sensation and memory. Bergotte dies in a gallery before Vermeer's *View of Delft*. Swann too passes away. Charlus, for the benefit of Morel, invites esteemed guests to attend a recital *chez* Verdurin; the force of art powerfully resurfaces as the Narrator hears for the first time a septet by Vinteuil, posthumously transcribed by his daughter's lover. The rudeness of Charlus and his guests prompts Mme Verdurin to take revenge, using deceitful rumours and slander to turn Morel against Charlus, who is publicly humiliated. The Narrator buys Albertine elaborate gowns by Fortuny; he claims he wants to separate, then argues otherwise. Jealous turmoil, speculative thinking and reflection on music and the structuring of works of art are tightly interwoven. As long as Albertine's possible deceptions occupy the Narrator's mind he is unable to set to work. He longs for Venice and a new start, decides categorically to make a final break with Albertine, only to learn from Françoise that she has packed her things and fled whilst he slept.

The Captive is a disquieting book, full of suspicion, distrust and suffering. At times, however, it promises something beyond this, pulses with beauty and insight that unknit our brows and send us soaring into the heights of artistic revelation. From the outset, the Narrator makes plain his position, referring to 'Albertine … with whom I was bored, with whom I was indeed clearly conscious that I was not in love' (*C*, 4; *P*, 1611). Such statements are frequent in *The Captive*, but not loving Albertine is not the same thing as no longer *needing* her and much of the volume is concerned with the ways in which the Narrator attempts to deal with this need, a need of assurance that her desires are not for other women. In sequestering Albertine, however, he gradually becomes as much a captive as she is, since his jealousy of her unknown habits and past acquaintances is like 'a phobia … capable of assuming as many forms as the undefined evil that is its cause' (*C*, 16; *P*, 1618). The enduring nature of his dilemma can be seen in the reformulations of this situation throughout the volume (jealousy is later described, for example, as 'a demon that cannot be exorcised, but constantly reappears in new incarnations'; *C*, 110; *P*, 1679).

In leaving Balbec, the Narrator had hoped he could distance Albertine from temptation. It quickly becomes clear, however, that so fixated is he on her possible infidelities that temptation, to his mind at least, is everywhere. Soon the terms used to describe their relation painfully reflect its growing awkwardness, the impossibility of tenderness or satisfaction: 'our engagement', as he memorably puts it, 'was assuming the aspect of a criminal trial' (*C*, 58; *P*, 1645). His problem is that he has to deal not only with the real manifestations of Albertine's desires, such as the tryst with Andrée that he almost intrudes upon, returning home with a bunch of syringas (*C*, 54–5; *P*, 1643–4), but also the host of imagined acts of passion, stolen glances and assignations that his mind tirelessly manufactures. The Narrator's suffering comes from the creative capability of his mind, not yet channelled towards art and thus free to work obsessively to formulate the destructive fables of jealousy. (Symptomatic of this is the striking regularity with which the word 'hypothesis' crops up in this volume.)

Albertine, multiple and mobile in Balbec, is, in Paris to quote just one page, 'caged' and 'cloistered' (*C*, 69; *P*, 1653). Her containment intermittently soothes the Narrator's suffering, caused by the thought of her desires being untrammelled; however, it also – crucially – dampens his desire. Excised from the magical maritime context of Balbec, Albertine, the 'glittering actress of the beach', becomes 'the grey captive, reduced to her drab self' (*C*, 191; *P*, 1732–3). The Narrator experiences the same phenomenon when he brings to his room a dairymaid who, seen from his window, had piqued his interest: up close, however, 'stripped of all the desires and imaginings that had been aroused in me, [she] was reduced to her mere self' (*C*, 156; *P*, 1710). Reality thus overpowers his imagination's illusion until the girl uses an unfamiliar name for a garment she wears and reveals that she rides a bicycle and wears a cap. As these details pile up we realize (even if the Narrator does not – he makes no mention of it) that this girl is not picked at random: she is an Albertine substitute. But, painfully for the Narrator, pretending to seek an address to which he must send the girl on an errand, he notices that at the Trocadéro, where he has sent Albertine in order to avert a meeting he suspects her of planning with Mlle Vinteuil *chez* Verdurin, Léa, the notorious lesbian actress, is playing the lead role in the main attraction (*C*, 157; *P*, 1711). This devastating news (did Albertine call his bluff, knowing that Léa was performing?) is rendered more bitter by the name of the play: *Les Fourberies de Nérine* is about the treacheries or deceptions ('*fourberies*') of Nérine, whose name has much in common with Al*bertine*, whose own deceitfulness causes the Narrator such suffering.

For all that he claims no longer to love Albertine, revelations (or what he assumes are revelations) of this sort wreak havoc with the Narrator's state of mind and constantly defer the possibility of his starting to write. Albertine's proximity and his constant involvement in her life become a habit and, as he acknowledges late in the volume, 'in love, it is easier to relinquish a feeling than to give up a habit' (*C*, 406; *P*, 1870). The conventional sense of the term 'love', already a little bruised from its handling in 'Swann in Love', takes a battering in *The Captive* (at one point the Narrator achingly notes 'here I mean by love reciprocal torture'; *C*, 117; *P*, 1684). Echoing Swann's experience, the Narrator describes love as 'an incurable malady' (*C*, 89; *P*, 1666) before expanding on what he perceives as the primary obstacle to his happiness:

> I realised the impossibility which love comes up against. We imagine that it has as its object a being that can be laid down in front of us, enclosed within a body. Alas, it is the extension of that being to all the points in space and time that it has occupied and will occupy. If we do not possess its contact with this or that place, this or that hour, we do not possess that being. But we cannot touch all these points. If only they were indicated to us, we might perhaps contrive to reach out to them. But we grope for them without finding them. Hence mistrust, jealousy, persecutions. We waste time on absurd clues and pass by the truth without out suspecting it. (*C*, 106; *P*, 1677)

In the simplest of terms, in this final sentence Proust highlights the fallibility that defines so many of our relations. Despite recognizing the impossibility of 'possessing' another person, the Narrator never manages to develop his conception of love beyond these terms, which are a significant limitation to his happiness. Even once Albertine has become 'a burdensome slave' of whom he wishes to rid himself (*C*, 424; *P*, 1882), his inability to possess a sure knowledge of where she has been, where, even, her desirous thoughts might have taken her, prevents him from making the decisive split that would grant them both their liberty. And so the tale shuttles back and forth between the *ennui* of intimacy and the fear of losing the 'fugitive being' whose presence is the unique salve to the Narrator's anxiety.

The only time that he experiences unalloyed happiness in Albertine's company is when she is asleep: then all that is flighty and elusive about her is contained, her eyes closed to the world and to temptation. Unable to dissociate positive thoughts of her from the context in which they first met, the Narrator constructs a succession of sea-related metaphors to capture the experience of watching her, ultimately suggesting that he 'embarked upon the tide of Albertine's sleep' (*C*, 74; *P*, 1656). He feels that her sleep permits him a sort of holistic possession of her that he cannot have when they talk and he is obliged, as in society, 'to live on the surface of [himself]' (*C*, 71; *P*, 1654). Access to the deeper reaches of his self is normally possible only when he is isolated from others. For those who are jealous, however, isolation, as *The Captive* frequently shows, can be as tortuous as the company of the person who provokes their jealousy: even when we are alone, 'associations of ideas, memories, continue to act upon us'. Nevertheless, when Albertine leaves the apartment, the Narrator is 'revivified … by the exhilarating virtues of solitude' (*C*, 19; *P*, 1621): looking out on to the new day, he somehow reconnects with the latent musicality of his soul, which is set vibrating by the promise of the outside world.

And it is music that repeatedly provides hope beyond the stifling relationship in which the Narrator is trapped. First there is the experience of hearing the street criers below his window, their motley instruments and the tools of their trades offering a sort of '"Overture for a Public Holiday"' and their intermingled cries forming a sort of secular liturgy, a plainchant intoned by hawkers and pedlars (C, 124–38; P, 1689–99). The parts of the Narrator's personality that he identifies at the start of the volume as likely to survive all others, 'a certain philosopher who is happy only when he has discovered between two works of art, between two sensations, a common element' and the 'little mannikin' similar to the one in the Combray optician's window, who responds to changes in the weather (C, 4–5; P, 1611) are active in this scene, predominating for once over his jealous self. Later on, liberated by Albertine's absence and soothed by the certainty of her return, the Narrator takes the opportunity to apply his thoughts to Vinteuil's sonata. Within moments he plunges to the heart of his aesthetic concerns ('was there in art a more profound reality', he asks, 'in which our true personality finds an expression that is not afforded it by the activities of life?'; C, 174; P, 1721). He compares the sonata to Wagner's *Tristan* and the impact suggests an affirmative answer to the question just posed: he senses an effect deep inside him, an experience of art's power that is visceral and profound. As so often in the *Search*, the consideration of one art form leads to a reflection on others: in this case the Narrator quickly moves from Vinteuil and Wagner to a mini essay on the late or retrospectively imposed unity of great works of the nineteenth century, drawing examples from Balzac, Hugo and Michelet (see C, 175–8; P, 1723–4).

The major revelation occurs *chez* Verdurin where, despite being in company, the Narrator has an experience that draws together art, creativity, memory and desire. Initially he does not recognize the music being played, then suddenly he finds himself 'right in the heart of Vinteuil's sonata' (C, 281; P, 1790). The piece is his septet, which owes its existence to the patient deciphering of old manuscript scores by Mlle Vinteuil's lover. The septet is Vinteuil's masterwork; in it aspects of the sonata the Narrator knows so well are dispersed and threaded through a larger, more complex structure. Proust's metaphor-laden account of the interpretive, rememorative and sensory processes that take place in the act of listening, simple yet wildly complex under analysis, is a remarkable achievement, a high point of *The Captive* and the *Search* as a whole. The relation the Narrator describes between the septet and Vinteuil's early work bears an intriguing resemblance to Proust's own writings: 'Vinteuil's sonata … and his other works as well, had been no more than timid essays, exquisite but very slight, beside the triumphant and consummate masterpiece' (*C*, 284; *P*, 1792). This situation is mirrored in the Narrator's amorous affairs to date, which, he realizes, 'were paving the way' for his love for Albertine. Conspicuous in all these scenes (the street sounds, playing the sonata, listening to the septet) is the word 'joy'. The Narrator's sentiments relating to Albertine are communicated largely in terms of suffering and anxiety, so when the word 'joy' repeatedly surfaces, we are reminded that he *is* capable of happiness, but that the most likely route to achieving it will not be through Albertine.

She is the Narrator's central preoccupation in *The Captive* and key events are often framed by or recounted in relation to developments in their relationship. This is the case with the death of Bergotte, another of the novel's peaks of intensity, where, in the shadow of the uncompromising finality of death, a life lived is weighed up against the achievements of art. Proust avoids sentimentalism and leads us, with poise and humour, between the heady raptures of art and the ineluctable indignities of dying (*C*, 207–9; *P*, 1743–4). When newspaper reports of Bergotte's death appear they contradict Albertine's story that the previous evening she had met Bergotte and spoken with him at some length. The Narrator does not suspect a thing at the time 'so artlessly had she described the meeting', for, as he puts it, 'it was not until much later that I discovered her charming skill in lying naturally' (*C*, 209–10; *P*, 1744). It is important to note, however, that Albertine is by no means the only liar in the relationship: the Narrator very often lies or says the opposite of what he thinks in order to provoke admissions or revelations from Albertine. The lesson learned, with time, is that truths are always revealed, but seldom when one is actively pursuing them.

Bergotte's death takes a prominent place in the narrative, as we might expect for the writer whose novels comforted the Narrator like the embrace 'of a long-lost father' (*SW*, 114; 84). As *The Captive* progresses, a number of deaths (such as those of Princesse Sherbatoff and Mme de Villeparisis) are mentioned, dropped parenthetically into conversation by socialites eager not to dwell on the past for fear, perhaps, of having to acknowledge the finite nature of their own existence. Saniette ill-advisedly speaks critically of Morel's performance to M. Verdurin, receives a ferocious dressing-down and is made to leave, whereupon he has a debilitating attack from which he never fully recovers (*C*, 802–3; *P*, 1802–3). Subsequently Charlus is humiliated by rumours and insinuations spread spitefully by Mme Verdurin, peeved at the ungracious attitude of his guests and greatly fearful of losing to Charlus and his set Morel, 'her' musician and a valuable asset in her social ascent. This accumulation of unpleasantness, added to the picture of the vulgar Verdurins sketched first in 'Swann in Love' and developed in *Sodom and Gomorrah*, results in an image of the couple as not only crass and self-interested but also cruel and callous.

After the soirée, however, readers are challenged by an account of how the Verdurins actually *helped* Saniette, ruined by gambling, after his stroke. Until his death and unbeknownst to all but Cottard, who told the Narrator the tale at Saniette's funeral, M. Verdurin provided him with an income which he was led to believe had been left to him in Princesse Sherbatoff's will. Suddenly we are faced with an unexpected side to M. Verdurin, with which we are ill prepared to cope. The Narrator reflects that: 'it is as difficult to present a fixed image of a character as of societies and passions. For a character alters no less than they do, and if one tries to take a snapshot of what is relatively immutable in it, one finds it presenting a succession of different aspects … to the disconcerted lens' (C, 373; P, 1849). The lessons in perspective and point of view, begun with Elstir on the first trip to Balbec in relation to visual art and the physical environment, are still ongoing, now expanding into the social and moral spheres. These comments reveal the Narrator's maturing outlook and prepare us for similar episodes late in *The Fugitive* and in *Time Regained* where Saint-Loup's homosexuality is exposed and Charlus's taste for sado-masochism is discovered.

Before then, at the Verdurin soirée, we see how, as Charlus has aged, aspects of his character, particularly his sexuality, have become more pronounced, almost to the point of caricature. The Narrator says of Charlus that 'he recognized immediately things to which no one would ever have paid attention, and this not only in works of art but in dishes at a dinner-party (and everything else between painting and cooking)' (C, 247; P, 1759), remarks which remind us of the similarity between Charlus and the mature Narrator himself. Indeed, as we learn more about Charlus and Morel's relationship we recognize troubles resembling the Narrator's own. Charlus's concerns about a salacious letter from Léa to Morel that he accidentally opens, however, equally recall Swann's turmoil over Odette's letter to Forcheville in 'Swann in Love'. Proust shows us how love affairs, whatever their nature, tend to take similar paths, stimulate the same emotions and insecurities, and in almost every case we blunder on, happily blinded by our desires to the fate that awaits us. There is a tension, then, between this point and that illustrated by M. Verdurin's unexpected compassion towards Saniette: relations and loves often unfold in the same patterns, yet individuals' characters are unpredictable, endlessly shifting. Proust does not seek to resolve this tension: he delights in observing how life can leave us perplexed or delighted by unforeseeable twists and turns just as often as it can pitch us into despair by taking a course which is familiar but over which we have no control. Drawing our attention to such matters, Proust invites us to revisit our earlier assessments of people and situations, wills us to look more carefully, to judge less quickly.

The closing movement of *The Captive* draws away from the salons and brings us back into the enclosed spaces shared by the Narrator and Albertine. When he arrives home, he pauses to look up at Albertine's window, lit from within: behind the 'parallel bars of gold' formed by the light escaping the slats of the shutters, the Narrator is aware that there lies a treasure, but one 'in exchange for which I had forfeited my freedom, my solitude, my thought'. Proust's language recalls the conceits of the metaphysical poets: these bars have the semantic value of precious metal and carceral confinement; Albertine is enclosed yet the Narrator feels entrapped: 'I seemed to behold the luminous gates', he suggests, 'which were about to close behind me and of which I myself had forged, for an eternal slavery, the inflexible bars of gold' (*C*, 378; *P*, 1852). Joy for the Narrator – and for Albertine – is a long way off, and something between them has to give.

His jealous inquisitions resume, provoking lies and unexpected revelations in equal measure. The floodgates yield when Albertine loses her temper and lets slip part of a phrase whose full sense the Narrator, like a frustrated crossword puzzler, takes a long time to piece together. Albertine cries that she wishes he would leave her 'une fois libre pour que j'aille me faire casser …' (*P*, 1857) [free for once so that I can go and get myself b…] (*C*, 385, trans. mod.). The expression that the Narrator eventually realizes, with shock and dismay, had been on Albertine's lips is 'me faire casser le pot', an extremely vulgar slang phrase meaning 'to have anal intercourse'. Albertine's language has always been a source of fascination and pleasure for the Narrator; now her words represent a gateway to an abject world whose existence he has suspected, but the reality of which, for reasons of self-preservation, he had not fully countenanced.

This verbal wound for the Narrator is a deep one. His reaction is to suggest that they separate the following day. In the conversation that ensues things deteriorate as Albertine, in a bid to prove a commitment to honesty, admits that she once had a three-week holiday with Léa. The Narrator's metaphor for the impact of this admission is a forceful one: 'I watched a tongue of flame seize and devour in an instant a novel which I had spent millions of minutes in writing' (*C*, 399; *P*, 1866). Despite his mental turmoil, when it comes to the moment of action, the Narrator cannot bring himself to split from Albertine: he play-acts a reconciliation and they agree to renounce the plan to separate. Reflecting on this episode, the Narrator's summary of his predicament puts one in mind of the tortuous situational dramas of Samuel Beckett, one of Proust's most sensitive early critics: the Narrator laments 'the impossibility of living together which is the cause of our daily suffering, a suffering preferred by us to that of a separation, which will, however, end by separating us in spite of ourselves' (*C*, 410; *P*, 1873).

A preoccupation of the Narrator's since the earliest stages of the *Search* is Venice; repeatedly in *The Captive* he alludes to the fact that Albertine's presence prevents him from fulfilling his dream of visiting the city. He delights in the Fortuny gowns he buys Albertine, whose designs borrow motifs from paintings by Carpaccio and Titian, thus layering the artistry of the contemporary designer with that of the Renaissance painters. The bewitching multiplicity of these garments has its downside, however: the reminders of Venice they provide make the Narrator feel his 'captivity' in Paris all the more sharply.

As the winter gives way to spring his desire for Venice increases, shifts in the weather once more influencing his own mental readiness for change. Before his decision comes, however, there occurs a final positively inflected scene, a last glimmer of hope before we are hauled through the fraught and frantic pages of *The Fugitive*. This scene bears close examination for it offers us once again a model of interpretive practice that we might apply to our reading of the *Search* and beyond. Albertine sits at the pianola and plays pieces of music for the Narrator several times over, knowing from habit that he likes in this way gradually to piece together the disparate lines of the works' structure. Once again we find our keyword: 'She knew and, I think, understood the *joy* that my mind derived … from this task of modelling a still shapeless nebula' (*C*, 425; *P*, 1883; my emphasis). Like the Narrator in this scene, often the best approach to the *Search* is to apply these principles of careful, repeated appraisal; so doing, in time, the work's internal structuring, cross-currents and echoes become more familiar, more accessible. Listening to Vinteuil in this way affords the Narrator the realization that the joys of great art can approximate to those he felt tasting the *madeleine* or seeing the shifting bell-towers at Martinville: the artist's apprehension of the world, the impression it makes on him or her, is communicated, transposed into art and projected to listeners or viewers through it (*C*, 426–8; *P*, 1884–5). Here we have the beginnings of the Narrator's theory of art, which will have its full expression in the library scene in *Time Regained*. For now, however, these pleasures are fleeting and the promise of an artistic vocation unfulfilled, for the Narrator's captive soon becomes a fugitive

The Fugitive

The fraught pages of *The Fugitive* tell of the Narrator's coming to terms with Albertine's disappearance. Each of his many selves must, in turn, adapt to his new circumstances. He constructs and unpicks seemingly endless hypotheses regarding the motivations for her departure and takes solace from bringing young girls to his apartment, a habit that earns him a police summons.

Saint-Loup is sent to scout for Albertine in the Touraine where her aunt has a house. She spots him, however, and writes to the Narrator, claiming to be willing to return provided he cease his underhand tactics. He attempts, unsuccessfully, to call Albertine's bluff and make her return. Eventually he sends her a despairing plea but it crosses with a message from Mme Bontemps informing him of Albertine's death in a riding accident. His jealous enquiries, through Aimé, and his tortuous self-scrutiny and repeated revisiting of their shared past, however, continue well after her death. Gradually his state of mind improves, he begins to notice other women again, in particular one whose allure seems tinged with familiarity: it is Gilberte, bearing Odette's new husband's name, de Forcheville. Hope that an artistic vocation may still be achieved comes when *Le Figaro* publishes an article by the Narrator. A trip to Venice with his mother reawakens him to the joys of art; simultaneously he begins to conceptualize a world without Albertine at its core. He learns of Gilberte's marriage to Saint-Loup and, soon after, through hearsay, of the latter's concealed homosexuality. Time spent with Gilberte at Tansonville and further revelations of Robert's character lead the Narrator to a retrospective reassessment of people and relations long taken for granted.

Albertine's departure poses the Narrator the problem of coming to terms with life on his own. Readers will recall his distress as a child, left without his mother's kiss. The solace derived from Albertine's kiss and her presence was associated with those of the mother in *The Captive*. Now the pain of Albertine's flight, he suggests, brings 'all the anxieties I had felt ever since my childhood … to amalgamate themselves with it in a homogenous mass that suffocated me' (*F*, 483; *AD*, 1923). This final verb (Proust's French gives 'étouffer') recalls the entrapment of the previous volume but equally serves as a reminder of the respiratory problems from which Proust suffered throughout his life and anticipates the increased use of images of illness and medicine we find in this volume. Even as gradually the Narrator discovered Albertine's lies and infidelities, her presence consoled him. Now in her absence his mind carries on its jealous fabulations without respite. Persuading himself that their separation will be temporary is harder than expected, since 'at every moment there was one more of those innumerable and humble "selves" that compose our personality which was still unaware of Albertine's departure and must be informed of it' (*F*, 490; *AD*, 1927). If this complexity were not enough, there comes the further realization that, like him, she is multiple: even after the death of her physical being she lives on in manifold forms in his memory.

As a result, major themes of *The Fugitive* are suffering, solitude, memory and the multiplicity of human character. Geographically speaking, this volume is wide-ranging, taking in Paris, Venice, Balbec and the Touraine. Nevertheless, the landscapes to which readers have to become accustomed for long stretches are those of the Narrator's mind. For the most part we are enclosed with the thoughts, vivid and wild, of the Narrator. Coming to terms with Albertine's departure involves rethinking his relation to moments of his past, for after her disappearance (and above all after her death) their relationship exists only in his memories. *The Fugitive*, as a result, might be considered as the archive or memory of the novel up to that point: for the Narrator to be able to move beyond his loss and overcome his anxieties, he must reconsider past incidents, often long distant, and put his past selves (and the multiple Albertines to which they are attached) to rest. Voluntarily and involuntarily, many moments return to the Narrator's mind, sparking his thoughts and challenging our reading memory. He realizes that forgetting, oblivion (the French '*oubli*' has both these senses) is what he needs in order to move on; but, just as we cannot voluntarily call to mind all our past experiences, we cannot *will* oblivion to submerge our past: forgetting takes time and before the period of calm which this eventually brings must come pain; and *The Fugitive* has this in abundance.

When Françoise matter-of-factly observes that Albertine's rings, discovered in a drawer, seem to come from the same source (something Albertine had denied), the Narrator's reaction illustrates a recurring concern of *The Fugitive*, the painful interrelation of mind and body. It is not just a mental torment he suffers: 'I might have picked up the wrong bottle of pills and, instead of swallowing a few veronal tablets on a day when I felt that I had drunk too many cups of tea, might have swallowed as many caffeine tablets, and my heart would not have pounded more violently' (*F*, 530; *AD*, 1953). This analogy shows how the force of mental activity, here the thought that Albertine was 'kept' by another person, can assail our vulnerable bodies with little warning. The Narrator's moments of greatest joy arise from the conjunction of his bodily, sensory engagements with the world (with a scent, a flavour, a certain musical signature) and the mental activity they provoke (such as a flood of memories or a rush of happiness then expressed through metaphors for the experience itself). The destabilizing impact of finding these rings is a reminder of the negative and potentially damaging nature of the mind–body relation to which the Narrator is so sensitive. As the volume progresses we encounter many more images of troubled or disturbed interactions between mind and body which remind us how coming to terms with loss is both mental *and* corporeal.

The following comment, made after hearing of Albertine's death, reveals how out of synch the Narrator's emotions are with the events he has just learned about: 'for the death of Albertine to have been able to eliminate my suffering' (that is, the suffering caused by her lies, infidelities and her departure), he reflects, 'the shock of the fall would have had to kill her not only in Touraine but in myself. There, she had never been more alive' (*F*, 546; *AD*, 1963). He superficially takes cognizance of her death (the phrase 'Albertine was dead' and variants on it occur repeatedly in the pages that follow, as if to show his attempts at acceptance) but he cannot face this reality, let alone mourn her, until his jealous preoccupations are worked through. And they are legion.

Her death makes little initial difference to the Narrator's state of mind: after all, the mental images we have of someone do not differ greatly according to whether that person is alive or dead; it is impossible 'to picture to ourselves anything but life' (*F*, 594; *AD*, 1995). But often these pictures are painfully vivid: when Aimé reports back on Albertine's liaisons with a girl who worked in a bath-house she frequented, his messages are all too detailed and feed yet another round of anguished imaginings, built upon Albertine's phrase 'oh it's too heavenly!' (*F*, 600; *AD*, 1999), uttered in the throes of passion. Additionally, in the course of his daily business, the Narrator's actions provoke involuntary memories of Albertine that offer a curious blend of pleasure (past happiness is relived) and pain (from the realization that the Albertine and the self remembered are no more):

> occasionally, as one recovers the remnants of a squandered fortune, I recaptured ['retrouvais'] some of them [happy memories of Albertine] which I had thought to be lost ['perdus']: for instance, tying a scarf behind my neck instead of in front, I remembered a drive which I had never thought of since, during which … Albertine had arranged my scarf for me in this way after first kissing me. (*F*, 607; *AD*, 2004)

Lost and found, the past as treasure: word and image choices here subtly recall the goals of the *Search*, announced from its title page. Perhaps, the optimistic reader might think, spotting these keywords, there *is* a way out of the labyrinth, a spark of hope beyond the Narrator's lengthy ponderings in the dark.

Approaching the close of Chapter One, he refers to his 'waning love', alludes to the possibility of new amorous adventures; but, predictably, he soon suggests that taking lovers is merely an attempt to fill a vacuum that cannot be filled. He had earlier reflected in an uncompromising (not to say breathtakingly misogynistic) moment that 'there is not a woman in the world the possession of whom is as precious as that of the truths which she reveals to us by causing us to suffer' (*F*, 567; *AD*, 1977). By the end of the chapter, his suffering does seem to have brought him to a point of relative stability and lucidity. His mind, characteristically, is already reaching beyond Albertine to the formulation of a law that might hold for all relations. What is salutary for self-preservation in the short to medium term (he will forget Albertine and be able to get on with his life) is negative in the long run because of the implications it has for emotional interaction and 'love' more generally: 'it is the tragedy of other people', he summarizes, 'that they are merely showcases for the very perishable collections of one's own mind … one bases upon them projects which have all the fervour of thought; but thought languishes and memory decays' (*F*, 637; *AD*, 2024). And so, staggering under the heft of this gloomy observation, we pass on to Chapter Two.

'It was not that I did not still love Albertine', he begins, and we wonder whether there will be any end to his vacillations. He realizes that he must make the retrograde journey through the different phases of his love in order to arrive at his 'initial stage of indifference' (*F*, 638; *AD*, 2024), a phrase which recalls the opening lines of 'Place-names: The Place', in *Within a Budding Grove*, where he confidently announced having 'arrived at a state of almost complete indifference to Gilberte' by the time of his first trip to Balbec (*BG*, 253; *JF*, 511). He is aware (and careful, retentive readers will remember) that he has been through this process before: it was his renewed indifference to Gilberte that allowed him to pay heed to the young girls at Balbec in the first place.

Out walking one day he finds himself humming Vinteuil's sonata in which, towards the end, the notes of the little phrase become dispersed. This takes on a new significance: 'aware that, day by day, one element after another of my love was vanishing … it was my love that, in the scattered notes of the little phrase, I seemed to see disintegrating before my eyes' (*F*, 640; *AD*, 2026). On the same walk he catches sight of a group of young women whom he tries, unsuccessfully, to follow. Seeing them again leaving the Guermantes' doorway a few days later, the Narrator is 'set aflame' by the lingering gaze of one of them. A note from the Guermantes' concierge reveals her name to be Mlle Deporcheville, which he 'corrects' to 'd'Éporcheville', the young woman of high birth who Saint-Loup had informed him frequented houses of assignation. To confirm he has the right name, he sends a telegram to Saint-Loup, only to receive, after a spell of frantic anticipation, the deflating news that the woman they had spoken of was 'Mlle d'Orgeville', at present out of the country: his excitement has been for nought. A little later, *chez* Guermantes, the girl who had caught his gaze asks to be *re*-introduced to the Narrator. The mistaken name was *de Forcheville*, that of Odette's second husband, Swann's old rival, now adopted by Gilberte. The girl whose allure he had keenly felt but who he had not recognized is his childhood friend, now 'one of the richest heiresses in France'. 'Our mistake', states the Narrator, reflecting on the sequence of events and echoing lessons learnt long ago from Elstir's paintings in Balbec, 'lies in supposing that things present themselves as they really are, names as they are written, people as photography and psychology give an unalterable notion of them' (*F*, 656; *AD*, 2036).

Between Saint-Loup's telegram and the discovery of the alluring stranger's identity there intervenes an episode which is a key step on the Narrator's path towards becoming an artist. His article (the piece on the Martinville bell towers we read in *SW*, 217–18; 149–50) appears in a newspaper, *Le Figaro*. Suddenly we enter an extended, detailed consideration of artistic production and consumption. The Narrator seeks to read it as if he were not the author (an impossible task but not one we are surprised to find him attempting). In short he tries to piece together a phenomenology of reading, a philosophical account of the nature of the act itself, similar to the consideration given to the act of listening to music in *The Captive* when the Narrator first hears Vinteuil's septet. Commenting that the beauty of a written text is partly in the author's thoughts and 'fully realized only in the minds of his readers' (*F*, 652; *AD*, 2033), he anticipates an important strand of twentieth-century literary theory, paradigmatically expressed in Roland Barthes' key essay 'The Death of the Author' (1968).[5] He also comes to the vital realization that writing might free him from his numbing worldly obligations: through writing he might wean himself off hollow social pleasures and find real satisfaction in literature (*F*, 654; *AD*, 2035).

Andrée, questioned at length in the first chapter, is grilled once more; having admitted to same-sex relations but denied they ever took place between her and Albertine during her first questioning, she now admits having previously lied. Her revelations – of the intricacies of the syringa incident; of assignations arranged between Morel and Albertine, where young girls were lured and corrupted by the former, then turned over to the desires of the latter; of liaisons, earlier categorically denied, in the Buttes-Chaumont and elsewhere – are, curiously, not entirely negative for the Narrator. They cause the pain associated with discovering unpalatable truths, but they also afford him the pleasure of seeing his jealous suspicions proved correct after a long spell of uncertainty. Repeatedly *The Fugitive* seems to tell us that the truth always hurts, but it is not without recompense since it tends to lead us towards a better understanding of the greater laws that determine our behaviour.

The process, however, is long and slow, and the world-weary Narrator is able to conclude at the close of Chapter Two only that 'truth and life are very difficult to fathom', a statement whose simplicity of sentiment and syntax contrasts strongly with the convolutions of so much of what we have laboured through to arrive at this point. Sad and exhausted, he embarks upon his long-anticipated journey to Venice with his mother. Finally his indifference towards Albertine seems complete: he explores the enchanted streets and canals of Venice, halfway between land and sea, evocative of Combray and Balbec, a city of art and the near-constant promise of erotic fulfilment. Previously multiplicity of

character, of appearance, of behaviour (for example, the Martinville bell towers; the sea at Balbec; Odette; Charlus; Albertine) has introduced complexity
and uncertainty. Now in Venice, multiplicity and mutability seem to be the
norm, a source of delight, revelation and beauty. Changes in the tides conceal
or reveal unexpected aspects of ancient buildings; as the waters and levels of
sunlight shift, the historic city takes on a host of colourings and atmospheres in
which the Narrator delights – maritime yet urban, familiar yet strange, exotic,
Byzantine, ancient yet vibrantly alive and alluring.

His mother's tenderness, the contemplation of art and architecture, and the
promise of the abundant and (he imagines) willing young women of Venice,
often metaphorically tied to the art of the city (such as the seventeen-year-
old glassware seller whose 'beauty was so noble, so radiant, that it was like
acquiring a genuine Titian before leaving the place'; *F*, 735; *AD*, 2087), seem to
have displaced Albertine from the Narrator's mind. Then one day a telegram
arrives, which reads 'you think me dead, forgive me, I am quite alive, I long to
see you, talk about marriage, when do you return? Affectionately. Albertine'
(*F*, 736; *AD*, 2088). Although we might expect such news to cause an unprecedented upheaval, it comes at a time when, in his mind, Albertine is now quite
dead, so the emotional impact of the news is negligible. He realizes that she
was 'no more … than a bundle of thoughts' and now that those have dissipated
like the notes of the little phrase, nothing can reignite his earlier feelings. He
feels that this impression confirms the 'total … death of [his] former self' and
a 'complete … substitution of a new self for that former self' (*F*, 736–7; *AD*,
2088). A genuine sea change seems to have occurred, although careful readers
have cause for scepticism: the telegram that seems to announce Albertine's
resurrection is far from incontrovertible: the message is tainted by 'corrup-
tions introduced by the Italian clerks' and is 'filled with inaccurately transmit-
ted words' (*F*, 736; *AD*, 2088). Like the handwritten note from the concierge
earlier on, this is another example of the Narrator, so ponderous in arriving at
conclusions under other circumstances, taking at face value a message whose
possible fallibility he would do well to question.

He mentions a 'work on Ruskin' in which he is engaged – further evidence
of a turn towards a productive occupation. Immersion in the art of Venice
aids his progress in re-establishing himself post-Albertine, but an involuntary
memory relating to her threatens his new-found calm when he notices in a
Carpaccio painting a figure wearing a garment on which was modelled the
Fortuny cloak Albertine wore on their last trip together. This unexpected link
to his past restores to the Narrator 'the eyes and the heart of him who had set
out that evening with Albertine for Versailles' (*F*, 743; *AD*, 2093). Past time,

we realize once again, is not static or dormant: it is volatile and apt to burst forth into our present should we happen across the right trigger, the existence of which we might be quite unaware. The desire and melancholy the memory instils in him last only a few moments but as he and his mother prepare for their departure from Venice a new problem, a sort of existential inertia, takes hold of him.

With their luggage already dispatched to the station, he sees in a list of guests due to arrive the name of Mme Putbus, the woman whose maid he has longed to meet since being tipped off about her by Saint-Loup (*SG*, 109–11; 1280–2). He announces he will stay on in Venice; his mother departs, hoping he will join her at the station when he comes to his senses. He eventually does, but first he yields to a crisis which has been waiting to spill over since Albertine's disappearance. Unleashed by the thought of the carnal pleasures with the chambermaid that his departure will make him forgo, feelings of frustration, purposelessness and above all isolation circle round the baleful Narrator, carried on the notes of the hotel singer's rendition of 'O Sole Mio', which seems to pull apart the city around him and his relation to it, leaving him stranded, rudderless.

He finally composes himself and makes it to the station just in time. On the train the Narrator opens a letter he received before leaving the hotel. It is from Gilberte, revealing that the telegram purporting to be from Albertine was in fact from her, the flourishes and embellishments of her handwriting leading 'Gilberte' to be transcribed by telegraph operator as 'Albertine'. The tendency towards error inherent in our interpretive efforts is laid bare here: we rely on the accurate deciphering of written and spoken messages in every sphere of our lives yet our hermeneutics – our art of interpretation – is far from being an exact or reliable science. As the Narrator sums it up: 'we guess as we read, we create; everything starts from an initial error; those that follow (and this applies not only to the reading of letters and telegrams, not only to all reading), extraordinary as they may appear to a person who has not begun at the same place, are all quite natural' (*F*, 754; *AD*, 2099). Proust's novel celebrates the achievements of art and the revelations of memory; crucial passages like this remind us that it also derives great nuance from its exploration of errors and misconstruals, which often prove to be highly valuable for the would-be artist and the reader of the novel alike.

The focus of the final chapter moves away from the Narrator's mental travails and on to the marriages of Saint-Loup to Gilberte and of Legrandin's nephew to Jupien's niece who now bears the noble title 'Mlle d'Oloron', conferred upon her by Charlus, her adoptive guardian. The ironies and absurdities provoked by such restructurings of the societal landscape are duly noted: because of her title, when Jupien's niece, 'a simple little seamstress', dies from typhoid soon after her wedding, it 'plunges all of the princely families of Europe into mourning' (*F*, 774; *AD*, 2111).

Following the news of Gilberte's marriage come rumours of Saint-Loup's homosexuality (*F*, 762; *AD*, 2104). When he hears a little later that Robert is thought to be keeping mistresses, the Narrator has his own suspicions; Jupien, then Aimé, helps to confirm his hunch: Robert's marriage is one of duty and form, and vitally linked to Gilberte's fortune. She eventually discovers a letter addressed to Robert, signed 'Bobette', who the Narrator discovers to be Morel, on whom Robert spends great sums of Gilberte's money. Her uncertainties regarding the letter replay her father's when faced with Odette's letter to Forcheville; they also recall Charlus faced with the letter from Léa to Morel, which referred to him in the feminine, a gender shift mirrored in the signature 'Bobette'. Proust tightens the screw yet further: Robert is attracted to Morel because he resembles his ex-mistress, Rachel (whose name anagrammatically is found in 'Charlie'). Robert asks Gilberte to dress as a man, leaving one lock of hair free at the front to resemble Morel, a request that recalls Gilberte's mother's transvestism in the *Miss Sucripant* painting, whilst Gilberte, unaware of Robert's preferences, seeks to please him by dressing like Rachel. The patterns of recurrence and return that shape all the novel's relationships reach their apogee in these pages. The Narrator's position in this wretched echo-chamber is one of sadness and disappointment, not because he is judgemental of Saint-Loup's choices but because he has lost a friend: now that men arouse Saint-Loup's desires, they 'no longer inspire his friendship' (*F*, 791; *AD*, 2122).

The Narrator does, however, grow closer to Gilberte. Through her, he renews links to his past in Combray. Spending time together at Tansonville, he discovers that past habits and assumptions had veiled realities quite different from what he had believed to be true as a boy (the source of the Vivonne can be found; the two ways, Guermantes and Swann, can be taken in on the same walk; Gilberte did in fact love him when they played together and desired him again upon seeing him from the Guermantes' porch when he took her for Mlle d'Eporcheville).[6]

The Fugitive tests our readerly resilience as we work through the Narrator's neurotic search for closure on his relationship; it tests our powers of recall and brings back into focus many disparate episodes of the *Search*, drawing together many of its narrative threads. And it shows us how contingency and desire are forces far more influential than the powers of the analytical mind that seeks to account for and contain them.

Time Regained

Amongst the revelations of the Narrator's stay with Gilberte at Tansonville is a strong sense that he lacks literary talent. Ill, he spends years in a sanatorium, visits Paris for a brief spell in 1914 and returns in 1916, but these episodes are not narrated in chronological order. We hear first of his impressions of the city in 1916, fashion trends and the new composition of society. We then return to 1914 and Saint-Loup's and Gilberte's respective, revealing accounts of the impact of the war. Jumping forward again two years, the Narrator strolls with Charlus while the latter expounds his particular, pro-German world view. They part ways; seeking respite the Narrator eventually finds a hotel run, it transpires, by Jupien as a male brothel. He voyeuristically witnesses Charlus chained and flogged by a hired thug. The scene is enfolded in reflections on desire and morality. Saint-Loup is killed in action and soon Morel is arrested for desertion. The Narrator retires once more to a sanatorium, returning to Paris only after the war. Unable to work, he decides to attend a society matinée. En route he meets Charlus, a link between different periods of the Narrator's existence but now frail and much deteriorated in health. A succession of involuntary memories suddenly revitalizes moments from his past, which he had thought forever inaccessible. With these fleeting extra-temporal experiences, he realizes that the life he has lived can provide the material for a work of art which might help to acquaint others with their own inner depths. The matinée reveals how the social kaleidoscope has turned: Mme Verdurin, by remarriage, has become the Princesse de Guermantes; the two ways of Combray are joined in Gilberte and Saint-Loup's daughter. All around are intimations of mortality: old acquaintances are transfigured by age, bodies and memories are damaged by the passage of time, but the Narrator must hold firm: his imperative now is to write.

The final volume opens without fanfare. After further revelations of Saint-Loup's infidelities (to Gilberte's great chagrin he does keep mistresses, although she ignores that it is not for pleasure but to divert attention from his homosexual affair with Morel), we find the Narrator settling down with some bedtime reading on his final night at Tansonville. As so often in the *Search*, a mundane activity proves to be highly revealing. In a recently published volume of the Goncourt journal he reads an account (incorporated in the text and in fact a brilliant pastiche of the journal) of a dinner *chez* Verdurin attended by Edmond de Goncourt in the company of Swann, Cottard, Brichot and others already familiar to us. The journal's effect on the Narrator is profound. When he attended such dinners, he found the guests insipid, the conversation banal. Goncourt's version of events suggests quite the opposite. It makes the Narrator question his own capacity for observation, the likelihood of his ever being able to write. He had felt that literature was intended to illuminate the deeper truths of the human condition, yet here it is crammed with crockery design, potato salad and chatter about discoloured pearls. If this is literature, thinks the Narrator, either I am not destined for it, or it is not what I had thought. The crux of the matter, as Elstir had announced long before with regard to painting, comes down to vision and perspective. Without fully recognizing the advantages of such an approach, the Narrator notes that when in society, rather than soaking up surface detail *à la* Goncourt, his attention is drawn to how individuals' manners of speaking 'revealed their character or their foibles'. Rather than looking at guests at a dinner party he 'was in fact examining them with X-rays', seeking a knowledge deeper than that afforded by table talk and appearances (*TR*, 33–4; 2147). For now the Narrator feels that 'Goncourt knew how to listen, just as he knew how to see; I did not' (*TR*, 37; 2149). When he finally recognizes and outlines the goals of his own work of literature later on, it becomes clear how his radiographic approach *is* well suited to revealing truths about life, far beyond what Goncourt's writing could ever achieve.

After Tansonville the Narrator mentions the 'long years – in which I had … completely renounced the project of writing which I spent far from Paris receiving treatment in a sanatorium' (*TR*, 39–40; 2151). With this the narrative winds forward to his return in 1916. The city is changed by the coming of war and the passage of time; the social ascension of Mme Verdurin and Mme Bontemps, for example, is such that they are described as the 'queens of this wartime Paris' (*TR*, 40; 2151). By 1916 it was already a decade since Dreyfus's pardon and reinstatement in the military: so long, in the memory of the little clan, that Brichot refers to the period of the Affair as '"those prehistoric times"' (*TR*, 45; 2155). Mme Verdurin now says '"Come at 5 o'clock to talk about the war" as she would have said in the past: "Come and talk about the Affair," or … "Come to hear Morel"' (*TR*, 49; 2157). However much they vaunt their sentiments with regard to the war, for these socialites so doing is just another otiose occupation, like playing cards or listening to music. The contrast between the Paris of the wealthy non-combatants and the situation experienced at the front is poignantly underlined when 'a wretched soldier on leave' is described looking into the windows of a packed restaurant, just as the working-class locals gazed into the restaurant at Balbec; the Narrator, reflecting on this man's imminent return to the trenches, imagines him saying to himself '"You'd never know there was a war on here"' (*TR*, 54; 2160).

The realities of the war, however, do make their way into the narrative. We hear that many of Saint-Loup's contemporaries from Doncières perished at the battle of the Marne and elsewhere (*TR*, 64; 2166). Gilberte writes to the

Narrator in September 1914 telling of her experience of fleeing the raids on Paris for her safety, making it back to Tansonville, only to find herself obliged to billet German troops. Robert, serving at the front, writes around the same time, voicing dislike for the clichés of nationalism but also burgeoning admiration and respect for the men around him and under his command (*TR*, 77; 2175). A second letter from Gilberte in 1916 shows how circumstances can change the way we perceive and recall things. In this letter, forgetting the earlier one, she claims that she originally returned to Tansonville not to escape the dangers of the raids but to save from the advancing German troops the estate that had been so dear to her father. She describes how in the 'battle of Méséglise' the places of their childhood became strategic sites in a key military conflict: the hawthorn path was the dividing line between French and German troops who, for over a year, each held half of Combray. The 'deux côtés' or two sides that shaped the Narrator's childhood conception of time and space are absorbed into the narrative of the war and take on a new complexion.

Focus then shifts to Charlus, who the Narrator, out walking, identifies as the shadowy figure he sees following a pair of *zouaves* (infantrymen from Algeria) in the streets at dusk. He now bears little resemblance to the *grand seigneur* we first met in Balbec: shamed and ridiculed *chez* Verdurin in *The Captive*, he still suffers from a universally bad reputation. Morel publishes slanderous articles about him and Mme Verdurin seeks to discredit him any way she can, spreading rumours that (amongst other things) he is a German spy (*TR*, 93; 2184–5). Charlus does have Germanic origins (his mother was Duchess of Bavaria) and he happily makes his pro-German opinions known but, as the Narrator points out, this does not make him immoral, merely unpatriotic in a country where patriotism frequently spills over into blinkered jingoism.

Proust's portraiture is a constant source of entertainment and insight throughout the *Search*. Mme Verdurin, readers will recall, is captured unflatteringly in *The Captive*, her nose greased with rhino-gomerol to protect her from the impact of Vinteuil's music (*C*, 271–2; *P*, 1784); in *Time Regained* we have another rather unsavoury snapshot. Despite shortages, to calm her headaches she obtains a spurious prescription from Cottard permitting her to have croissants made for her breakfast. The first of these 'medicinal' pastries arrives the morning the newspapers report the sinking of the *Lusitania*, an ocean liner torpedoed by a German U-boat in May 1915, taking over 1,000 lives:

> "How horrible!" she said … But the death of all these drowned people
> must have been reduced a thousand million times before it impinged
> upon her, for even as, with her mouth full, she made these distressful
> observations, the expression which spread over her face, brought there
> (one must suppose) by the savour of that so precious remedy against

headaches, the croissant, was in fact one of satisfaction and pleasure.
(*TR*, 102; 2190)

Whilst remaining non-judgemental, the single sentence of commentary here
gives us all the detail we need to recognize the depth of disingenuousness, self-
centredness and moral apathy in Mme Verdurin.

By contrast, on just the following page we read of the 'rare moral qualities'
of Charlus (*TR*, 103; 2191), who criticizes at length the biased presentation
of the conflict in the newspapers, vital organs of communication in times of
war. Charlus shows more compassion and feeling than Mme Verdurin can
muster for fellow human beings when he relates to the Narrator the fate of
the Combray church. Structurally, thematically and symbolically important
as a site of continuity between past and present (*SW*, 68–75; 55–60), it was
'destroyed by the French and the English because it served as an observation
post to the Germans'. Charlus laments the destruction of 'all that mixture
of art and still-living history' (*TR*, 130; 2207); when Saint-Loup is killed his
body is returned and buried at Combray, an addition to the line of illustri-
ous Guermantes whose presence below the ground contributed to the 'four-
dimensional' feel of the church when it still stood.

Having parted ways with Charlus (*TR*, 147; 2218), the Narrator walks on,
but, fatigued, seeks somewhere to rest before returning home. One establishment in the almost deserted streets shows signs of life: an officer leaves
whose face the Narrator does not see but whose gait is very similar to Saint-
Loup's. The conversation he overhears of the men sitting in a room near the
door offers scant interest until mention is made of someone being tied up and
beaten. Keen to satisfy his curiosity and his thirst, he enters 'with the pride of
an emissary of justice and the rapture of a poet' (*TR*, 150; 2220).

The hotel, it soon transpires, is a male brothel. The talk of those inside the
establishment, mainly working-class men and servicemen on leave, offers a
counterbalance to the views of the war we have already encountered from
Charlus and Saint-Loup. After taking a room and having a drink, the Narrator
creeps upstairs out of curiosity. 'Stifled groans' emanate from the room he
finds there. Peering in through a small, fortuitously un-curtained window,
he sees the recipient of the blows, 'chained to a bed like Prometheus to his
rock': Charlus (*TR*, 154; 2223). He has visible bruising from previous beatings
and very real blood runs down his back, but this scene, like many others in the
Search, is about illusion and desire. Jupien enters – he is the proprietor of the
establishment, the Narrator-voyeur discovers – and Charlus hectors him about
his assailant, Maurice, who is neither 'sufficiently brutal' nor suitably convincing in his verbal abuse (*TR*, 156; 2224). Jupien offers the services of a man
from a slaughter house and, when this individual enters, the Narrator notices

that both men vaguely resemble Morel. Just as the Narrator and Saint-Loup sought satisfaction in the arms of others resembling their lost loves, Charlus seeks a substitute satisfaction at the hands of men who look like his inaccessible object of desire. Maurice and the slaughter-man, however, are in fact a jeweller's assistant and a hotel worker, playing roles under Jupien's direction to fulfil the baron's fantasy. Afterwards, when Charlus performs a sort of inspection of Jupien's employees, it becomes clearer still how far his satisfaction is determined by his imagination: Jupien swears his men are thugs, murderers and pimps, which pleases Charlus, but when one denies he would kill a woman and another says he will share his payment with his parents and his brother at the front, remarks that suggest underlying virtue, Charlus cannot contain his angry disappointment.

There is a commotion at the hotel about a *croix de guerre* that has been found. An air-raid delays the Narrator's return home, but on his arrival he finds that he has missed Saint-Loup, who called in looking for his missing medal: progressively, it seems, the paths of uncle and nephew converge in their pursuit of pleasure, an endeavour which for so many of the novel's characters takes precedence over all other concerns. Before leaving Jupien's hotel the Narrator witnesses an obstreperous client demanding the services of a particular employee for the following day, enraged at the thought that anything might come between him and his pleasure. Soon after, however, we encounter two characters who contrast starkly with this particular pleasure-seeker.

Françoise's cousins made millions as café proprietors before taking retirement; when their nephew dies in the war, leaving behind his own café to run and a young widow, they come out of retirement, getting up at dawn for three years to work through the day for no other reward than seeing their niece kept afloat. When this anecdote is related, Proust's voice intrudes:

> In this book where there is not a single incident which is not fictitious, not a single character who is a real person in disguise, in which everything has been invented by me in accordance with the requirements of my theme, I owe it to the credit of my country to say that only the millionaire cousins of Françoise who came out of retirement to help their niece …, only they are real people who exist. (*TR*, 191; 2246)

Society might have its share of 'vile shirkers' like the arrogant man at Jupien's hotel (we might equally think of croissant-munching Mme Verdurin) but 'they are redeemed', the Narrator argues, by the 'innumerable throng' of selfless, compassionate people like Françoise's cousins the Larivières whom he puts on a par with the soldiers defending their country (*TR*, 191–2; 2246). This unexpected authorial intercession draws attention to the novel's fictional status and warns readers off interpreting it as a *roman à clefs*; it might, moreover, be seen as an effort from the author to emphasize his support for the national cause in the wake of criticisms he received as a non-combatant when *Within a Budding Grove* won the Goncourt prize in 1919.

The Narrator retires to another sanatorium and 'many years' pass before he returns to post-war Paris by train (*TR*, 202; 2253), a journey we might see as closing the loop begun with the first exultant trip to Balbec that saw him dashing back and forth, trying 'to obtain … a continuous picture' of the shifting skies at sunrise (*BG*, 268; *JF*, 521). His return to Paris, however, is without such promise; from the train he gazes on a sunlit stand of trees but derives no pleasure from their beauty: 'if ever I thought of myself as a poet,' he glumly comments, 'I know now that I am not one' (*TR*, 202; 2253). He is convinced his life has been for nought. The name of the Princesse de Guermantes on an invitation to a matinée, however, reignites for him memories and associations of past times, which convince him to emerge from his seclusion.

Against the void of his recent experiences, on the way to the reception he suddenly feels himself soaring 'towards the silent heights of memory': threading the Paris streets he took with Françoise on his way to the Champs-Élysées as a boy, his carriage seems to be transporting him through various layers of his past (*TR*, 206–7; 2255–6). Stopping en route he meets Charlus, white-haired, physically diminished but still lucid. Charlus's listing of contemporaries who have died underscores a key theme of the novel's closing movement: 'every time he uttered it, the word "dead" seemed to fall upon his departed friends like a spadeful of earth each heavier than the last' (*TR*, 212; 2259). Death sinks us into the earth, inanimate, whilst memory permits us to soar to vertiginous heights; the turbulence we experience between these positions is explored by Proust in the remaining pages of the novel.

Stepping aside to let a carriage pass in the Princesse de Guermantes' courtyard the Narrator stumbles on some uneven paving stones. This physical sensation disperses his discouragement and gloom, fills him with the same, sudden pulse of happiness provoked by the bell towers at Martinville, the taste of the *madeleine*, the experience of hearing Vinteuil's septet. He soon recalls having the sensation before in St Mark's Square in Venice, the memories of which flood back just as had those of Combray with the *madeleine*. In the pages that follow, the Narrator has a succession of further experiences of involuntary memory. A spoon knocking against a plate recalls the sound of a railwayman's hammer on the wheels of the train in which he sat and observed, unmoved, the row of sunlit trees on his return to Paris; wiping his mouth with a starched napkin brings back the seascape at Balbec that he looked upon, drying his face with a similarly textured towel, on his first morning there; the shrill sound of water in a pipe recalls the pleasure-steamers at Balbec; and discovering a copy of *François le Champi* in the library reincarnates in him the young boy who first read the book with his mother in Combray. The pages dedicated to working through the many lessons of these experiences are some of the richest and most densely packed in the novel; they repay close attention and re-reading.

When experiencing the past and the present at once, that moment, strictly speaking, is neither: it is situated outside Time. For their fleeting duration these moments offer a sense of eternity – time in its purest, immeasurable state. Impressions are stored up within us, often 'lost' in the depths of our memories without our being aware of it. If we happen to encounter the right trigger we can relive the original experience in a very pure form, unadulterated by the deformations our mind can introduce when we seek consciously to store an impression. The Narrator states that 'the impression is for the writer what experiment is for the scientist, with the difference that in the scientist the work of the intelligence precedes the experiment and in the writer it comes after the impression' (*TR*, 234; 2273). The writer's inner store of impressions is a book that he or she alone must learn to decipher before finding a way to transform impressions into expressions – a written form that communicates to the reader.

Merely describing things as the Goncourt journal does cannot perform this task, for 'it is only *beneath* the surface of [what] such a literature describes that reality has its hidden existence' (*TR*, 253; 2284; my emphasis). Metaphor is key to accessing this 'hidden existence': to interpret a metaphor we must identify an underlying commonality or essence in two things. Through metaphor we get away from mere description and into relationality and interconnection, the pluralities of the world which have fascinated the Narrator throughout the novel.

His experiences can be used to create a work of art which thereby redeems or makes good on the life previously thought worthless. The work in turn offers its readers the opportunity better to recognize life's riches; it is likened to an optical instrument with which we might 'read ourselves' (*TR*, 273–4; 2296–7) and avoid the superficiality that otherwise renders so much of our lives '*temps perdu*'. These ideas, and many more that there is not space to consider here, swarm forth from the Narrator's mind, finally channelled into creative matters beyond jealousy, mourning and illness. If Proust's theory of literature emerges from these pages in a rather ragged manner, it has every reason to: the suddenness of the Narrator's epiphanies has provoked a fervent hyperactivity of mind; a neater, more regimented statement from our author-to-be would be out of keeping with the spontaneous rush of the whole episode. We should also note that the editing of *Time Regained* was not finished before Proust's death, which may account for some of the repetition and inconsistency found in the text.

As he moves into the salons, the tone and focus shift. The guests seem to be masked or disfigured travesties of the old and ageing. But there is no illusion: these are the effects of time on the human body. Time has stooped and silvered individuals who in the Narrator's mind were still in their prime. He is by no means immune but it takes some time for the realization of his own ageing to sink in. These pages offer counterbalance to the euphoria of the triumph over time by which the Narrator was gripped in the library: now frailty and the ultimate threat of death are everywhere in evidence. He feels ready to start his work but also increasingly aware of the limited time he has left to complete it.

At the matinée he is confronted with what he terms 'the sensation of Time' (*TR*, 317; 2321), which reveals a disadvantage in the way our memories store up images and impressions: 'nothing is more painful', he summarizes, 'than [the] contrast between the mutability of people and the fixity of memory' (*TR*, 372; 2355). We may be able fleetingly to experience moments outside time but we can do nothing to halt its progress: bodies grow weak, memories grow feeble, details and dates are forgotten, the past becomes '*temps perdu*'. Time, however, is not only destructive:

> Life is perpetually weaving fresh threads which link one individual and one event to another, ... these threads are crossed and recrossed, doubled and redoubled to thicken the web, so that between any slightest point of our past and all the others a rich network of memories gives us an almost infinite variety of communicating paths to choose from. (*TR*, 428; 2388)

If we try diagrammatically to link up even a handful of episodes or characters in the *Search*, the tangle of criss-crossing lines that result – 'transversals', Proust calls them (*TR*, 427; 2387) – vouch for the cogency of these remarks. An art that can incorporate this dense interweave and keep us alert to its nuances has a chance of counteracting the drain of forgetfulness from which everyone comes to suffer, the destructive force of time.

In the closing pages the tempo increases, the focus shifting away from the Narrator's acquaintances on to the business he feels will occupy him until he breathes his last. We are never told that the work we have been reading is that which the Narrator is about to begin writing. Proust's novel is not a closed circle (unlike Ian McEwan's *Atonement* (2001) in which the protagonist reveals herself in the novel's final section as the author of what has come before) and this open-endedness contributes to the urge to start over again that surprises many readers at the end of the book.

Appropriately enough for a work of its scope, the *Search* ends on an image of giants: our store of experience mounts up beneath us as we age, elevating us until in later life we totter as if on stilts, 'like giants plunged into the years' (*TR*, 451; 2401). Characteristically this image does not aggrandize its author: Proust's focus is on the wonder of the individual, the untold depths each of us has concealed within the meagre confines of our bodies. Our task now, aided immeasurably by Proust's book, is to sound those depths while we still have time

Proust criticism

'Impossible to make head or tale of it!' commented Jacques Normand (Madeleine was a fortuitous pseudonym), one of Proust's first critics, in the reader's report that led to the rejection of an early version of *Swann's Way* by the publishing house Fasquelle in 1912.[1] Despite serious misgivings, Normand concluded his report remarking that 'it is impossible not to see here an extraordinary intellectual phenomenon.'[2] And this phenomenon has attracted a staggering volume of critical responses (many more positive than Normand's) ever since. In 1992, Antoine Compagnon, in his informative overview of Proust's work and its fate through the years in France and abroad, published in Pierre Nora's *Les Lieux de mémoire* [*Realms of Memory*], estimated there to be 'certainly more than two thousand' books on Proust and his work.[3] Recent bibliographical data show that over 1,200 further books, articles and essays on Proust and his work were published between 2004 and 2008. The ever-growing secondary literature on Proust dwarfs the works on Montaigne, Balzac or Sartre.[4] So where does a beginner begin?

Getting started

There are several useful reference works we can lean on while reading Proust's novel. Terence Kilmartin's *A Guide to Proust* (1983), now published together with *Time Regained* in the Vintage edition of the novel, offers indexes of fictional characters; historical persons; places; and, usefully, themes, all with brief descriptions and fully cross-referenced. This makes tracking down particular passages easier and reminds flagging memories of relations and connections that may have grown fuzzy over time. In French, the fourth volume of the *Pléiade* edition has similar indexes which make navigating the text easier, with the additional benefit of listing all the works of art referred to in the novel. Readers will find much to enrich and enliven their reading in David Ellison's recent *A Reader's Guide to Proust's 'In Search of Lost Time'* (2010), in which he works through the novel volume by volume. Further help is at hand in the shape of the invaluable *Dictionnaire Marcel Proust* (2004), an amazing mine of information, with entries by specialists on topics ranging from motifs and characters in the *Search*, to biographical details of Proust's acquaintances and contemporaries, assessments of individual volumes and summaries of critical responses.

Beyond the solace of these reference works lies the daunting, varied terrain of Proust criticism. An excellent starting point is the *Cambridge Companion to Proust* (2001) edited by the late Richard Bales: here, fourteen essays from leading scholars offer appraisal, critique and analysis of a wide range of issues, from the novel's socio-cultural context to the role of the unconscious; comedy; the fine arts; and the unexpected pleasures of Proustian *brevitas*. Read together, these essays offer a solid grounding for any student of the novel; each one opens on to a whole sub-field of criticism, and there is a good bibliography.

Jean-Yves Tadié's *Proust: le dossier* (1983, various reprints) is still an extremely valuable resource from the general editor of the 'definitive' *Pléiade* text and author of the superlative French life of the author. Tadié offers a general overview of Proust's novel, the context of its production and its major preoccupations, before giving brief analyses of Proust's writings and the broad trends in the reception of the *Search*. Tadié's immense learning and familiarity with all things Proustian have more recently been distilled into a much shorter volume, whose grand title, *Proust: la cathédrale du temps* [*Proust: the Cathedral of Time*] (1999) rather belies its diminutive dimensions: in just over 100 pages, Tadié weaves a narrative of the life and work around beautiful illustrations of the places and people of Proust's life, as well as photographs of the fascinating excesses of the manuscripts and corrected typescripts In a similar vein and on a similar scale, Mary Ann Caws' excellent *Marcel Proust* (2003), in the 'Overlook Illustrated Lives' series, gives a wonderful sense of the colourful influences and inspirations that contributed to the production of the *Search*, supported by plentiful illustrations of works of art that Proust admired and that feature in the *Search*.

There are many options open to readers wishing to move beyond relatively brief introductory works. The historically minded should stop first at *Marcel Proust: The Critical Heritage*, edited by Leighton Hodson (1989), which features, in English translation, reviews and responses to Proust's work, from *Les Plaisirs et les jours* through to excerpts of the first critical studies of the *Search* from the 1930s. It contains a good number of pieces from the 'Hommage à Marcel Proust' number of the *Nouvelle Revue Française* that appeared in January 1923, including reflections from contemporary authors and critics, such as Gide, Thibaudet, Joseph Conrad and Ernst-Robert Curtius

Early studies

Many responses to the *Search* as it first appeared recorded timid admiration tempered by scepticism or wariness to praise too highly a work whose ultimate direction and endpoint were far from clear. A number of insightful, early studies stand out, however, written very shortly after the novel's publication was completed and which still offer substantial rewards to readers today. Among these are Walter Benjamin's essay 'The Image of Proust' (1929), Samuel Beckett's short monograph *Proust* (1931), and Edmund Wilson's chapter on Proust in his book *Axel's Castle* (1931). Benjamin's essay is remarkable for the ground it covers in less than fifteen pages and its capacity to move, like Proust, from the macro to the micro and vice versa. Just two years after the publication of *Time Regained* Benjamin already perceives that 'the eternity which Proust opens to view is convoluted time, not boundless time', whilst also remarking that 'Proust's pointing finger is unequalled'.[5] Beckett's book is erudite, cryptically allusive at times, but rewarding in its treatment of time, habit, memory and death – themes that later would become Beckett's own. He comments on Proust's 'perspectivism',[6] the multiplicities at work in the narrative. The study has a candour and a proximity to its subject that still makes for rewarding reading as much for what it reveals of the young Beckett as it does of Proust. Wilson's book considers Proust as part of a constellation of twentieth-century writers, alongside Yeats, Valéry, Eliot, Joyce and Gertrude Stein, who represent for him a culminating moment in the symbolist movement. The essay on Proust insightfully addresses structural issues in the narrative as well as Proust's presentation of love and sexuality ('[the *Search*] is one of the gloomiest books ever written').[7] Where Beckett refers to Proust's perspectivism, Wilson draws on the sciences and describes his achievements of incorporating *relativity* into the novel as being on a par with contemporary discoveries of modern physics.

Rewarding general approaches

Further, later studies complement the insights of these early luminaries with a longer view of Proust's practice as a novelist. Leo Bersani's *Marcel Proust: The Fictions of Life and of Art* (1965) still has abundant insights to offer readers, remaining particularly sharp on Proust's presentation of love, desire and pleasure and the psychological tensions explored therein. William Carter's *The Proustian Quest* (1992) is an engagingly written study of the goal-driven nature of Proust's novel, its argument illuminated by rich reference to the scientific and technological advancements of the *belle époque* as well as to a wealth of biographical information. Amongst general or introductory studies that take in the novel's full span, the best is Malcolm Bowie's prize-winning *Proust among the Stars* (1998). In thematically arranged chapters ('Self', 'Time', 'Art', etc.), Bowie reads the fine details and rhythms of Proust's text, just as he tracks long-distance plotting and echoes, with great subtlety and panache. Bowie sets Proust the multifaceted thinker resonating with figures as diverse as Ovid, Shakespeare, Luis Buñuel and Wallace Stevens. He is attuned to dissonance and fragmentation in a text often treated as a closed system and provides a powerful reminder that the novel's closing movement is as much concerned with the threat of death as it is with the idea of redemption through art.

Landmarks

As readers become more familiar with Proust criticism they will begin to note a number of names and titles that repeatedly crop up. In the space I have here I will outline a few of these enduring, strong readings of the *Search*, which provide a great deal of stimulating analysis to nuance and perhaps challenge readers' interpretations of Proust's novel. Chronologically first and highly influential is Gilles Deleuze's *Proust et les signes* [*Proust and Signs*], published in 1964. Deleuze subsequently appended additional sections to the work, the 'complete' edition appearing in 1970. For Deleuze the *Search* is about the Narrator's apprenticeship in reading the signs of intersecting domains: the empty signs of worldly interaction; the deceptive signs of love; material, sensory signs; and the essential signs of art which are capable of transforming all others. Deleuze's vision of the *Search* is of an assemblage of multiple parts, a heterogeneous weave of forward-reaching interpretive actions, rather than a neat, unified whole. His study prepares the ground in some ways for Bowie's *Proust among the Stars*.

Although he wrote no book-length study of the author, one of Proust's most gifted and sensitive readers in the 1960s and 1970s was Roland Barthes, whose strategies of reading and attitudes to textuality have left a profound mark on

Proust criticism and on literary studies more generally.[8] In his essays Barthes returns repeatedly to Proust, writing, for example, in 1974:

> Proust is a complete system for reading the world … There is not, in our daily lives, an incident, an encounter, a trait, a situation, without its reference in Proust: Proust can be my memory, my culture, my language … The pleasure of reading Proust – or rather re-reading him – resembles, albeit without holiness and respect, a biblical consultation.[9]

This statement is characteristic of the structuralist investment in the authority of the text ('Proust' in the sentences quoted surely stands for the novel to which he put his name). It is not all reverence and the Proustian sin of idolatry, however: 'the joy of Proust', writes Barthes elsewhere, 'from one reading to another one never skips the same passages.'[10]

Jean-Pierre Richard's *Proust et le monde sensible* [*Proust and the World of the Senses*] (1974) represents a major trend in French literary criticism of the period. It is an example of 'critique thématique' or thematic criticism, which minutely examines literary texts in order to map the workings of the writer's imagination. Richard draws on semiology (the science of signs) and psychoanalysis to build up a picture of how sense experience contributes to the construction of the imaginary world of the novel, gathering his explorations under the headings 'Matière' [matter], 'Sens' [meaning] and 'Forme' [form]. This seemingly simplistic approach reveals the complexities which the Narrator's own attention to simple things often unveils: 'When one reads Proust,' Richard comments, 'one is immediately struck by the extraordinary multiplication, variation, lability of both personal and sensory identities and by the importance of the hiatuses, the gaps separating each of their situations.'[11] When we look at the novel through Richard's optic our act of reading it is no dry academic pursuit, but a sensory encounter that leaves us longing to taste, to smell, to engage with the world around us. For Richard, the closer our attention to the text, the more we will learn about the inter-relation of the Narrator's sensations, intellect and imagination, all crucial for the production of the work of art. The revelations may not be neat, handle-able unities of sense but they tend to point towards something greater: as Richard memorably puts it, 'chez Proust, le décousu est toujours aussi l'en-train-de-se-coudre' [with Proust, what is disjointed is always also what is in the process of being joined up].[12]

Serge Doubrovsky's *La Place de la Madeleine: écriture et fantasme chez Proust* [*Writing and Fantasy in Proust: la place de la madeleine*], also published in 1974, is a bold study which reads the *madeleine* scene, its echoes and aftershocks, through the lens of Freudian psychoanalysis. Doubrovsky builds on the insights of Philippe Lejeune's important 1971 article 'Écriture et sexualité' [Writing and Sexuality]; the book offers a sustained example of the degree to which Freud's thinking about desire and sexuality can shed valuable light on the possible motivations of the complex narrative unfolding of Proust's novel. Malcolm Bowie's complementary *Freud, Proust, Lacan: Theory as Fiction* (1987) is a beautifully nuanced and subtle account of the overlap and interplay discernible between the kinds of thinking we find in Proust, Freud and his best-known French interpreter.

An extremely perceptive work that tackles many issues raised by Deleuze, Richard and Doubrovsky is Julia Kristeva's 1994 study, *Le Temps sensible: Proust et l'expérience littéraire* [*Time and Sense: Proust and the Experience of Literature*]. Kristeva's approach draws on genetic criticism (see below), psychoanalysis and a wide range of literary and philosophical sources. Like Doubrovsky her study begins with the *madeleine* but then gradually spreads outwards, taking in matters of character and characterization; sexuality and identity; speech, perception and metaphor; sensation and phenomenology; syntax and the experience of time. Kristeva's book expands and extends insights found in Richard and sets itself up explicitly in a position counter to that of Deleuze: 'il faut bien se résoudre à penser' she argues, 'que l'élément minimal de l'écriture proustienne n'est pas le mot-signe, mais un doublet: sensation et idée; perception représentée ou image incarnée' [we must resolve to think that the minimal element of Proustian writing is not the word-sign, but a pairing: sensation and idea; represented perception or incarnated image].[13]

Philosophy and fiction

Readers seeking further philosophical sustenance should consult Vincent Descombes' *Proust: philosophie du roman* [*Proust: Philosophy of the Novel*], published in 1987. Descombes observes that the Narrator's philosophical pronouncements, made when he is in theoretical or speculative mode, are less bold than those performed by the novel in which he appears. What Descombes explores, then, is whether we might uncover the 'philosophy of the novel' in narrative or descriptive passages, rather than those we might term explicitly philosophical; he sees the novel as a search not for lost time but for truth (here the philosopher and novelist share common ground). The book is an important exploration of the relation of philosophy to literature and the blurring of the boundary between them that we encounter in texts like Proust's.[14] A recent addition to this sub-field is Joshua Landy's *Philosophy as Fiction: Self, Deception and Knowledge in Proust* (2004) which, like Descombes and Beckett before him, focuses on Proust's perspectivism (Landy's reading of the Martinville bell towers scene is exemplary in this regard) as well as paying heed to the productive tensions at work between the philosophical and the literary within the novel. Landy's writing is accessible and his analyses sound, but Bowie's *Freud, Proust, Lacan* covers similar ground with greater finesse.

The relation between Nietzsche and Proust, which features in Landy's book, receives more detailed treatment in Duncan Large's *Nietzsche and Proust: A Comparative Study* (2001). Large focuses above all on issues of epistemology (questions relating to *knowledge*) and ontology (those relating to *being* and *existence*). He attends to the writers' respective attitudes to conversation, friendship and morality, and traces parallels between Nietzsche's notion of eternal return and Proust's use of metaphor and the functioning of involuntary memory. Mauro Carbone and Eleonora Sparvoli's *Proust et la philosophie aujourd'hui* (2008) is the most recent, important addition to the field, a rich collection including essays by Tadié, Compagnon and others on a wide range of philosophical and philosophically inflected topics. For a flavour of the field, readers should consult Anne Simon's essay 'The Formalist, The Spider, and the Phenomenologist: Proust in the Magic Mirror of the Twentieth Century', which offers a brief synthesis of the philosophical reception of Proust in France and appears in the volume edited by André Benhaïm, *The Strange M. Proust* (2009).

Style and narrative technique

The *Search* is a work of many voices, tones and rhythms. Proust's narrative techniques are many and varied. His is the work of an ironist, a *pasticheur*, a social observer and a humorist.[15] Brian Rogers' *Proust's Narrative Techniques* (1965), a revised, augmented edition of which appeared in 2004, traces developments in Proust's approach to narrative in his early writings before tracking the forms of perspective and focalization we find in the novel and how these determine its unfolding. Tadié's *Proust et le roman* (1971) covers similar ground; he focuses on the Narrator and Time, brilliantly scrutinizing their manifold, interconnected relations from which the architectural structures of the work emerge. The study of the narrative business of the novel is indelibly marked by the work of French structuralist Gérard Genette, whose essays 'Proust palimpseste', 'Proust et le langage indirect' and 'Métonymie chez Proust' are bite sized precursors to his bold 200-page systematization of narrative practice, 'Discours du récit' [Narrative Discourse: An Essay in Method], published in 1972 and illustrated throughout with examples from the *Search*. This founding work of narratology has been widely studied and played a large part in the dissemination of Proust's novel outside modern languages faculties.

Other important works in this sub-field include Victor Graham's *The Imagery of Proust* (1966), a comprehensive survey of the nature and function of Proust's figural language;[16] Jean Milly's *Proust et le style* (1970) and *La Phrase de Proust* (1975; reprinted 1983); and Leo Spitzer's brilliantly perceptive essay 'Le style de Marcel Proust' in his *Études de style* (first published in German in 1961). This last piece covers material germane to Malcolm Bowie's superb essay 'Reading Proust between the Lines' (printed in Benhaïm's *The Strange M. Proust*), itself a pendant to his earlier 'Proust and the Art of Brevity' in the *Cambridge Companion to Proust*. Bowie's essays encourage us to pay heed to what he calls the 'micro-movements' of the Proustian phrase and sentence, to the rhythms, echoes and cross-currents that often get lost in interpretations that favour grand schemes over fine details. Layering or 'superimposition' is Bowie's intriguing subject in Benhaïm's book. Both essays should be read by anyone about to undertake a critical commentary or write an essay on a given Proustian theme: they charge us with receptivity, encourage us to look, to listen, to read with the care Proust bestowed on his work; the rewards are many.

Proust and the arts

A major area of Proust studies is that concerned with the role of music, visual art, theatre and literature in his work. J. M. Cocking's essays 'Proust and Music' and 'Proust and Painting' are a good place to start,[17] as is Bowie's extremely rich chapter 'Art' in *Proust among the Stars*. Bales' essay 'Proust and the Fine Arts' in the *Cambridge Companion* gives a valuable overview. In a crowded field Antoine Compagnon's masterly 1989 study *Proust entre deux siècles* [*Proust between Two Centuries*] stands out. It is a valuable resource for readers interested in two voices that resound with some insistence through the *Search*: those of Baudelaire and Racine; it also draws music, painting and the works of other writers of the period into its purview. Compagnon's thesis is that what characterizes the *Search* and *Sodom and Gomorrah*, its pivotal central volume in particular, is its in-between-ness, temporally and aesthetically between the nineteenth and twentieth centuries. Persuasive comparative essays on Proust and Manet, Fauré and Huysmans, among others, demonstrate how the text's recurrent undecidability is characteristic of its status as classic. Such works of art, Compagnon argues, do not lend themselves to straightforward, unproblematic interpretations: they are disconcerting in *any present moment*.

On Proust's views on music and the role of music in his novel, J.-J. Nattiez's *Proust musicien* [*Proust as Musician*], published in 1984, is the key study.

Readers should also consult Edward Saïd's *Musical Elaborations* (1991), which discusses Proust's theorization of music with great sensitivity. Emile Bedriomo's *Proust, Wagner et la coïncidence des arts* (1984) offers a comparative account of these two 'totalizing' creators of imaginary worlds. More recently, Alex Ross has written engagingly about the role of Vinteuil's music in the novel, in the broader context of imaginary music in fiction: interested readers will be well rewarded by his *New Yorker* essay 'Imaginary Concerts' (24 August 2009).

The scholarship on Proust and the visual arts is vast. A recent, valuable and extremely handsome contribution to the field is Eric Karpeles' *Painting in Proust: A Visual Companion to Proust's 'A la recherche du temps perdu'* (2008), which reproduces all of the paintings referred to in the novel. The catalogue from the major 1999 exhibition *Marcel Proust: l'écriture et les arts*, edited by Jean-Yves Tadié, is a significant resource. Many scholars have studied Elstir's role and that of Proust's imaginary artists more generally, independently and in relation to living artists of Proust's era (see Michel Butor's 'Les œuvres d'art imaginaires chez Proust', 1964). Christopher Prendergast's essay 'Literature, Painting, Metaphor: Matisse/Proust' in his *The Triangle of Representation* (2000) is illuminating. On the art and architecture of Venice in the *Search* (and much more besides), Peter Collier's *Proust and Venice* (1987) is a stimulating guide, and Richard Bales' *Proust and the Middle Ages* (1975) takes readers even further back in time, exploring another layer of Proust's composite aesthetics.

Studies concerned with Proust and literature – his influences and borrowings, his relations to contemporary and canonical writers, his influence on subsequent generations – are legion. Dominique Jullien's *Proust et ses modèles: les 'Mille et Une Nuits' et les 'Mémoires' de Saint-Simon* (1989) is a revealing account of these two pervasive presences that undergird much of the *Search*. Some comparative studies seek to explore similarities or divergences of novelistic practice between Proust and his contemporaries or near-contemporaries (such as Sarah Tribout-Joseph's recent *Proust and Joyce in Dialogue*, 2009 or Hugues Azérad's *L'univers constellé de Proust, Joyce et Faulkner: le concept d'épiphanie dans l'esthétique du modernisme*, 2002), whilst others explore the presence of inter-textual relations between Proust's novel and other works (Annick Bouillaguet's *Marcel Proust: le jeu intertextuel* [*Marcel Proust: Intertextual Play*] (1990) outlines the relevant critical-theoretical thinking on these matters). Peter Brooks' recent essay 'Modernism and Realism: Joyce, Proust, Woolf' is a rewarding example of comparative criticism, deftly sketching the relation of his three named figures' approaches to representation in the context of two of the predominant currents of nineteenth- and twentieth-century literary history.[18]

Self, sex and society

Brian Rogers' chapter 'Proust's Narrator' in the *Cambridge Companion* is a good starting point on the question of 'self' in the novel, ditto the chapter 'Self' in Bowie's *Proust among the Stars*. Kristeva, Deleuze and Richard all contribute greatly to our understanding of the Narrator's character. Richard Terdiman's chapters on Proust (above all on 'Narration in *La Fugitive*') in *The Dialectics of Isolation: Self and Society in the French Novel from the Realists to Proust* (1976) are highly rewarding, subtle readings which point tellingly towards how Proust, unexpectedly perhaps, anticipates aspects of Beckett's writing. Bersani's *Marcel Proust: The Fictions of Life and Art* and Edward Hughes' *Marcel Proust: A Study in the Quality of Awareness* (1983) take us closer in to the nature of the Narrator's mind.

Proust's own sexuality and the representation of love and sexuality in his novel have long engaged critics and readers alike (Alison Finch's *Cambridge Companion* essay gives an admirable overview of 'Love, Sexuality and Friendship'). Recently William Carter has brought his biographer's expertise and his critical acumen to bear on the subject in *Proust in Love* (2006), although it is the biographical that predominates over the fictional in this particular study. J. E. Rivers' *Proust and the Art of Love: The Aesthetics of Sexuality in the Life, Times and Art of Marcel Proust* (1981) remains an important reference. An acute and theoretically inflected account of sexuality in its relation to Proust's aesthetics, touching on issues of subjectivity, gender and identity, is found in Emma Wilson's *Sexuality and the Reading Encounter: Identity and Desire in Proust, Duras, Tournier and Cixous* (1996). Rewarding accounts of homosexuality's various inscriptions in the *Search* are provided by Elizabeth Ladenson's *Proust's Lesbianism* (1999) and Emily Eells' *Proust's Cup of Tea: Homoeroticism and Victorian Culture* (2002). Most recently Michael Lucey has offered a highly compelling account of the interplay of same-sex desire and narrative practice in his *Never Say 'I': Sexuality and the First Person in Colette, Gide and Proust* (2006).

Michael Sprinker's *History and Ideology: 'A la recherche du temps perdu' and the Third French Republic* (1994) is a forceful Marxist account of the presentation of society in Proust's novel that illustrates the socio-historical import of this paradigmatically 'literary' text. Readers of French should also study Jacques Dubois's elegant, incisive *Pour Albertine: Proust et le sens du social* (1997). Dubois suggests that in Albertine we find a figure that permits Proust to explore sociality, to engage in a sort of experimental sociology, which is often ignored by those who see the *Search* straightforwardly as a *roman d'analyse*.

Essay collections

A number of volumes of essays dedicated to Proust exists, such as *The Strange M. Proust* mentioned above, which bring together papers by experts around a given theme or topic. Benhaïm's book considers the enduring strangeness and intrigue of Proust's work, sometimes lost from view when it is considered as being monolithically 'about', say, time or memory. *Proust in Perspective: Visions and Revisions* (2002), consisting of essays stemming from the millennial conference held at the University of Illinois at Urbana-Champaign (where Philip Kolb, editor of Proust's correspondence, spent his career and left a vitally important research collection), is another valuable source of insights. Topics broached include the editing of the correspondence; biographical issues; genetic approaches to specific episodes; inter-textuality; and the role of visual art and music. The volume I edited, *Le Temps retrouvé Eighty Years After/80 ans après: Critical Essays/Essais critiques* (2009) provides a rich and varied assessment of the culminating volume of the *Search*, including considerations of Charlus's role, the place of 'theory' in the novel, its critical reception and its 'afterlife' in Raoul Ruiz's filmic interpretation of 1999. Finally, the collected papers from Antoine Compagnon's 2006–7 Collège de France seminar have recently appeared as *Proust, la mémoire et la littérature* (2009), a volume whose sparkling essays bring new energy to long-studied topics.

Genetic criticism

Genetic criticism is one of the major developments in Proust studies in the last forty years. It concerns itself with how a literary work of art comes into being: its primary objects of study are manuscripts, typescripts, notes and drafts that reveal the stages of development a work goes through, between the writer's mind and the 'finished' version you hold in your hands. Marion Schmid's essay in the *Cambridge Companion* is an excellent place to start for an overview of the field. Scholars have been able to scrutinize Proust's manuscripts since their acquisition by the Bibliothèque Nationale in Paris in 1962. Of many studies to date that have mined the holdings in this collection, most accessible are Alison Winton (Finch)'s *Proust's Additions: The Making of 'A la recherche du temps perdu'* (1977), which explores the evolution of the novel during the war years and after, tracing how Proust's shifting preoccupations map on to the developments of the ever-expanding manuscripts; and Anthony Pugh's *The Birth of 'A la recherche du temps perdu'* (1987), which seeks to plot how the Narrator's struggle to find a form for his art relates to Proust's own challenges in the vital creative period of 1908–9, as he sought to manage his material and manipulate it into something resembling a novel. Specialists will long be consulting Pugh's vast follow-up study, *The Growth of 'A la recherche du temps perdu': A Chronological Examination of Proust's Manuscripts from 1909 to 1914* (2 vols., 2004), which undertakes the monumental task of giving a reasoned assessment of how the individual components (from whole notebooks to single sheets) of the huge corpus of materials from this period fit together.

In the field of genetic criticism, the status of the text of *The Fugitive* has been a major point of contention. In 1986 a typescript was discovered which bore corrections in Proust's hand that advised the excision of almost two-thirds of the narrative – most of the Narrator's detective work regarding Albertine's sexuality and her possible infidelities. Additionally, Proust had changed the place of Albertine's death from the Touraine to Montjouvain. The implications of this change are significant: if Albertine fled to Montjouvain, this suggests she was motivated by a desire to see Mlle Vinteuil and her friend again and so offers 'proof' of her lesbianism, thus obviating the need for intervening pages of speculation and reflection. The status of this typescript, however, is not clear. Nathalie Mauriac Dyer has argued that it was intended as final and published the resulting shorter version of *Albertine disparue* with Grasset in 1987. Jean Milly has argued otherwise and published a competing 'full' edition of the volume with Honoré Champion in 1992. The Vintage translation, 'Quarto' Gallimard and *Pléiade* editions of the novel print the fuller version of *The Fugitive*. For a concise yet thorough and engaging account of this controversy and the publication and reception history of Proust's novel more generally, Christine Cano's *Proust's Deadline* (2006) is highly recommended.[19]

Epilogue: Proustian afterlives

The idea that Bergotte was not dead for ever is by no means improbable. They buried him, but all through that night of mourning, in the lighted shop-windows, his books, arranged three by three, kept vigil like angels with outspread wings and seemed, for him who was no more, the symbol of his resurrection. (*C*, 209; *P*, 1744)

Almost a century after the publication of *Swann's Way*, and well over eighty years after his death, Proust undoubtedly lives on in the twenty-first century. Like Bergotte's, his books still keep vigil on displays in stores and shelves in libraries. Critics and commentators, journalists and bloggers mention his name, allude to traits of his work; opinions and *idées reçues* pass between generations of readers; and so, improbably yet perceptibly, in our modern, hurried world where verbal communication comes in 'tweets' rather than tomes, the man, the myth and the work live on. *In Search of Lost Time* continues to attract readers and provoke critical responses, but not solely in the form of scholarly articles, monographs and academic conferences. For many years Proust's face and appearance have been caricatured by cartoonists and illustrators in the broadsheets, literary journals and colour supplements. Since 1998 enthusiasts have been following and awaiting successive instalments of Stéphane Heuet's version of *In Search of Lost Time* in graphic novel format, of which five beautifully illustrated volumes have appeared to date.[1] Those wishing to be more demonstrative of their devotion to the author can wear their affiliation across their chest (or elsewhere) by going online and choosing from a range of inexpensive and readily available t-shirts, pin-badges, aprons, even underwear bearing stock quotations and, more often, the mustachioed visage of the author. Mugs, clocks, bumper stickers and various other items are similarly to be had at the click of a mouse.[2] On the Internet we find a good number of Proust-related blogs, offering discussion of the experience of reading (or re-reading) the novel; and in November 2009 a project was launched on the micro-blogging site Twitter, with the goal of rewriting the *Search* in a series of 140-character 'tweets' (progress can be followed at http://twitter.com/prousttweet). In the multimedia world, the writer and his work live on in a vast array of formats.

Beyond Proust's Internet and media presence, and his place in consumer society (call it cynical commodification or geek chic, either way the Proust 'brand' sells), there exists the Société des amis de Marcel Proust et des amis de Combray [Society of Friends of Marcel Proust and of Combray], which organizes workshops, lectures, book launches and suchlike. The Maison de tante Léonie-Musée Marcel Proust in Illiers-Combray is run under the Society's auspices and in summer visitors can follow a reading tour around the '*circuit-aubépines*' [hawthorns route]. The Society also publishes annually the French-language *Bulletin Marcel Proust* (formerly the *Bulletin de la Société des amis de Marcel Proust et des amis de Combray*, frequently referred to in the critical literature as *BSAMP*), which gathers the work of scholars associated with the Proust research centre at the *Université Paris 3 – Sorbonne Nouvelle*.[3]

Another important group, this time with a uniquely scholarly focus, whose work pushes Proust ever further into the new century, is the Équipe Proust [Proust Team] at the Institut des Textes et Manuscrits modernes (ITEM), a major research centre which works in association with the École Normale Supérieure in Paris.[4] These scholars work on Proust's manuscripts, proofs and other primary documents and publish the annual *Bulletin d'informations proustiennes*, which reflects the reassessments of Proust's novel and the explorations of his writing process afforded by genetic criticism; the latter part of the journal keeps readers abreast of Proust-related events and provides reviews of recent publications.[5]

A group of scholars, many of them from the Équipe Proust, is currently at work under the direction of Nathalie Mauriac Dyer on perhaps the biggest Proust project to date: a full facsimile edition of seventy-five of Proust's *Cahiers*, the notebooks from which the *Search* emerged: about 8,000 handwritten pages in all. Each *cahier* (two have appeared to date) is presented in two volumes: the first a stunning, digitally produced colour facsimile, in its original format, faced by diagrams of the '*unités textuelles*' [textual units] that make up each folio; the second is an exhaustive diplomatic transcription (that is, recording all annotations and deletions, every detail of Proust's palimpsestic pages as well as offering critical notes and remarks on chronology and interpretation). Together these volumes allow readers to explore the many-layered, multiform structures of Proust's writing, the likely order of composition of any given section, the movements of blocks of text and the addition of stuck-on strips and streamers of verbal matter in the age before word processing made such things possible at a keystroke. They remind us of the vast complexity of the tasks facing any editor seeking to produce a 'definitive' edition of the novel. These volumes are expensive, but when the project is completed (and it will likely take a generation or more), research libraries around the world will be able to offer readers an experience very close to that of consulting the original manuscripts themselves; at the same time this project will electronically preserve from further irreparable deterioration what are already fragile artefacts.[6]

Beyond the walls of the academy, artists of many stripes have drawn on Proust and his work for inspiration or creative stimulus. Film-makers have been attracted by the opportunities and challenges offered by the *Search* yet most have concentrated their efforts predominantly on a single volume of the novel. Volker Schlöndorff's *Un amour de Swann*, starring Jeremy Irons as Swann, Ornella Muti as Odette and Alain Delon as Charlus was released in 1984; Raoul Ruiz's *Le Temps retrouvé* (1999) features a galaxy of long-established stars, including Emmanuelle Béart, Catherine Deneuve and John Malkovitch (as Charlus); and Chantal Akerman's inventive drama *La Captive* appeared in 2000. Harold Pinter's 1972 *The Proust Screenplay* (first published in 1978) is the nearest anyone has come to a comprehensive filmic interpretation of the *Search*. The screenplay has never been made into a film but it was successfully adapted by Pinter and Di Trevis for the stage at the Royal National Theatre in London in 2000.[7] For an excellent overview of these and other filmic adaptations and responses to Proust's work, readers should consult Martine Beugnet and Marion Schmid's extremely valuable *Proust at the Movies*.[8] More recently, in their debut film *Little Miss Sunshine* (2006), starring Steve Carell as the United States' 'leading Proust scholar', Jonathan Drayton and Valerie Faris have unobtrusively woven Proustian concerns into a dark and bitingly funny scrutiny of a rapidly imploding family and the society of which they are part.

While Pinter's efforts intended for the big screen ended up on stage, Alan Bennett, another of Britain's finest playwrights, dramatized a brief period from Proust's life in an acclaimed television play, *102 boulevard Haussmann* (1990), which starred Alan Bates and offers an intriguing exploration of sexuality and artistic creativity.[9] Proust crops up with some regularity in Bennett's work: he is alluded to in *The History Boys* and, memorably, in his recent novel *The Uncommon Reader* (2007), among other treasures unearthed as she discovers the joys of reading, the Queen encounters Proust: 'really someone to whom one would have wanted to say, "O do pull your socks up."'[10]

In 1974, renowned choreographer Roland Petit created a ballet, *Proust ou les intermittences du cœur*, which was first performed in Marseille and is now part of the repertoire of the ballet of the Opéra national de Paris.[11] The work interprets the *Search* in thirteen tableaux, divided into two acts and danced to music by contemporaries of Proust, such as Saint-Saëns, Debussy, Hahn and Fauré, as well as by composers he admired such as Beethoven and Wagner; it is visually stunning, beautifully executed and revitalizes through movement and music many memorable moments of the *Search*, as well as its central preoccupation with desire and the erotic.

A radical vision of the *Search* has been staged in the Netherlands by Belgian director Guy Cassiers as a tetralogy amounting to a total performance time of around twelve hours. The first instalment premiered in Rotterdam in 2003 and the final part in 2005. The four parts of the cycle (*Swann's Way*, *Albertine's Way*, *Charlus's Way*, *Proust's Way*) draw on the *Search* as well as other sources, such as Céleste Albaret's memoir *Monsieur Proust*, and exploit video and audio technologies as much as they draw on the actors on stage. Often Proust's long sentences move from voice to voice between different actors; words and phrases are projected on to screens, sometimes alone, sometimes overlaid on top of images. The cycle uses a Flemish translation of Proust's novel as its script; a string quartet plays music by Debussy and Ravel, Webern and Kurtág: all in all this is a remarkably plural, multifaceted apprehension of the *Search* and one which has drawn large audiences in Rotterdam and on tour elsewhere in Europe.[12]

If these examples suggest a predominance of 'high-art' or 'high-brow' adaptations or creative apprehensions of Proust's work, there are many others that counter this trend. In 1979 *Dining with Marcel Proust* appeared, a book which presents, with adjoining quotations from the novel, recipes (among many others of the period) for dishes mentioned in the *Search*, so those wishing to translate the page on to the plate can recreate *sauce Gribiche* or *Nesselrode pudding* at their leisure (the culinary *cognoscenti* were earlier apprised of the *madeleine* moment by Elizabeth David in her 1960 classic *French Provincial Cooking*).[13] In the United States an off-Broadway musical based upon the Narrator's relationship with his beloved, *My Life with Albertine*, opened in 2003, including numbers such as 'My Soul Weeps' and 'I Need Me a Girl'. As in Cassiers's Proust cycle the question of perspective is addressed by having two actors, one older and one younger, play the Narrator.

In 1972 the third series of the cult British comedy show *Monty Python's Flying Circus* featured the 'All England Summarize Proust Competition', in which contestants have fifteen seconds to summarize the novel, first in swimwear, then in evening dress. For the curious and uninitiated, the sketch is readily accessible on YouTube, speculative searches of which fetch up many other manifestations of Proust's audio-visual afterlives. Those wanting to hear Proust *live*, as it were, can satisfy their desires on the first and third Thursdays of the month in the Librairie l'œil au vert in Paris's thirteenth arrondissement, where audiences gather to hear the Compagnie du Pausilippe, an association of public readers and storytellers, reading from *In Search of Lost Time*. At 8.15 p.m. the shutters are pulled down on the bookshop and, for their entry fee of €6, willing proustophiles can let his words wash over them without turning a single page.[14]

Alain de Botton's Proust-as-self-help guide, *How Proust Can Change Your Life* (1997) was a huge hit in the United Kingdom and the United States and has been translated into several languages, including French.[15] The burgeoning field of Proustiana saw two other notable contributions in 1997: Phyllis Rose's 'memoir in real time' entitled *The Year of Reading Proust* and Kristjana Gunnars' *The Rose Garden: Reading Marcel Proust*, a curious sort of 'autofiction' that reflects on the peculiarities of absorbing oneself in Proust's novel. More recently we have seen that even in the booming market of popular science writing, Proust's name helps sell more books. *Proust was a Neuroscientist* is the rather cynically catchy title of Jonah Lehrer's 2007 collection of fascinating essays on creative artists' anticipations of modern neuroscience.[16] Compellingly drawing on, amongst others, George Eliot, Proust, Stravinsky and Cézanne, Lehrer suggests that these great creative spirits of the nineteenth and early twentieth centuries might have facilitated more rapid developments in the sciences had their complementarity been recognized. Lehrer's insights are many and his book is a fine example of engaging, accessible, truly interdisciplinary research that successfully straddles and illuminates disparate fields. The fact that the book's title and the super-size *madeleine* that emblazons the cover wholly occlude the other excellent essays in the book shows how the Proust 'brand' sells like no other.[17]

A far less successful example (at least from a Proustian perspective) of attempted disciplinary border-crossing being sold under the sign of Proust is Maryanne Wolf's *Proust and the Squid: The Story and Science of the Reading Brain* (2007), which takes its cue from a brief paragraph in Proust's essay 'Days of Reading': enough, apparently to merit using Proust's name in the arresting title, despite there being no reference to him or his work in the 200 pages and more between the first chapter and the final paragraph of the conclusions. Wolf's discussion of the neuroscience of reading disorders and related matters is informative but Proust, who returns uneventfully in the book's penultimate sentence, is no more than a hook, a lure for potential readers who would not otherwise buy a book of science writing (squidophiles are only slightly better rewarded).[18] The glaring contrast with Lehrer's perceptive synthesis and analysis, his genuine interdisciplinarity (a trait we recognize everywhere in Proust's novel) is unforgiving. Germane to these examples of cross-fertilization in the humanities and sciences, readers curious about Proust's biography and the various ailments and pathologies that defined his adult life (and arguably shaped his world-view and hence his novel), should consult Brian Dillon's chapter on Proust in his *Tormented Hope: Nine Hypochondriac Lives* (2009).[19]

Dillon's study places Proust in a diverse pantheon of sufferers including Florence Nightingale, Charles Darwin and Andy Warhol: the constellations of creative minds in which Proust features (and often as the *ne plus ultra*) seem inexhaustible.

In the creative literature of the twentieth and twenty-first centuries readers will find many echoes and borrowings from Proust's novel. Critics have noted Proustian parallels in Sartre's *Nausea* (1938), for example, and throughout Beckett's writings.[20] Certain novelists are reminiscent of Proust in their use of imagery, their manipulation of time or their privileging of memory. Javier Marías' three-volume novel *Your Face Tomorrow*, for example (first published in Spanish 2002–7), has been widely praised and compared, on various levels, to *In Search of Lost Time*.[21] Among many examples in francophone literature one might consider Andreï Makine's *Le Testament français* (1995; English translation 1997), whose shifting narrative perspectives and treatment of memory has led commentators to remark its 'Proustian' qualities.[22] Orhan Pamuk's *The Black Book* (1990; first English translation 1995), whose central narrative thread of a man searching for his wife after her disappearance divides into a panoply of mini-narratives and searches for identity, truth and meaning, can be read as a re-writing of *The Fugitive*. Acknowledgement of this is made in one episode where the protagonist, Galip, describes a man for whom the 'only tremor in his quiet life was when Marcel Proust enticed him into reading *A la recherche du temps perdu*' and who, reaching the end of the book, returns to the beginning and starts over, spending the remainder of his life alone in his apartment, save for his cat, telling and retelling himself the story of the Narrator and Albertine.[23]

Diverging from this sort of homage, or the echoes found, say, in the writing about food and love in Jonathan Franzen's *The Corrections* (2001), or in John Banville's lexical precision, his imagery and handling of childhood and ageing, yoked painfully together by memory, in *The Sea* (2005), two novels stand out that offer a more overt and comprehensive 'use' of Proust in the creative process. Jacqueline Rose's *Albertine* (2001) is a fascinating, imaginative rewriting of Albertine's story, told from her perspective and that of Andrée.[24] The novel draws on scenes from Proust's fiction as well as his life; it shifts the dynamics of the *Search*'s central relationship and imaginatively makes heard voices often silenced by the Narrator. Like Rose's *Albertine*, Kate Taylor's *Madame Proust and the Kosher Kitchen* (2003) is a debut novel in which female voices dominate.[25] The tale of Marie Prévost, a young, modern-day Canadian who travels to Paris for a new start and explores the Proust manuscripts in the Bibliothèque Nationale is interwoven with 'translated' passages from the fictional diary of Proust's mother that she finds there as well as the story of Sarah Bensimon, the mother of the man from whom Marie fled to France, a Parisian Jewish woman sent to Canada to avoid capture during the war, who finds solace in later life by reproducing kosher versions of traditional French dishes. Taylor explores identity, memory and love across time and space in a complex, multifaceted narrative whose structures and thematic concerns have a distinctly Proustian flavour.

Less sustained but similarly inventive homage is found in Georges Perec's *35 Variations sur Proust*: these exercises in style, themselves a homage to Raymond Queneau, were originally published in a number of the *Magazine littéraire* devoted to the latter in 1974. Perec rewrites the opening sentence of Proust's novel whilst conforming to various constraints, ranging from anagrams to alexandrine metre: so doing he introduces readers to the tenets of the OuLiPo (*Ouvroir de littérature potentielle* – Workshop of Potential Literature), a group that makes a virtue out of formal constraints in the production of literary texts, and highlights yet again the multiplicities, the vast potential of even the briefest snippets of Proust's prose.[26]

While the Narrator ponders the afterlife that Bergotte's books represent for the author in *The Captive*, later in *Time Regained* when he himself is nearer to death he tempers this suggestion with the sober observation that eternal life is no more granted to works of art than it is to men. This may be so, but judging by the critical and creative responses, the varied cultural and commercial appropriations of the author and his work in the years – almost a century – since its publication began, we can safely say that Proust's mark is an enduring one. Proust may live on in contemporary culture because his work, as Margaret Gray has argued, stands gallingly for all that resists the very essence of that culture: 'In an age that values speed, brevity, efficacy, performance, and appearance,' writes Gray, 'Proust "signifies" slowness, length, labour, contemplation, resistance, transcendence.'[27] The preceding pages have shown many of the ways in which Proust's novel stands for these qualities, but they have equally shown how it has pace, brevity, flightiness and humour. Proust's conception of the primary concerns of his work – love, passion, identity, truth, happiness, mortality – may have taken shape in what is now a far distant, almost unrecognizable past. But the novel lives on for us today, providing shivers, laughs, tears and tired eyes because its concerns are enduring human preoccupations relevant to every and any epoch. As long as we continue to seek satisfaction, to love and deceive each other, to ponder questions of art, to search for happiness and an understanding of ourselves and the beauties of the world in which we live, Proust's novel, this singular, subjective rhapsody on experience, will continue to find an audience.

Notes

1. Life

1 The first questionnaire and responses are reproduced in William C. Carter, *Marcel Proust: A Life* (New Haven, CT and London: Yale University Press, 2000), pp. 52–3; Carter also discusses the second questionnaire (pp. 140–1).

2 For a full account of the (possible) meeting, see Carter, *Marcel Proust*, pp. 124–6 and, in French, J.-Y. Tadié, *Marcel Proust: Biographie* (Paris: Gallimard, 1996), pp. 158–9.

3 Letter to Mme de Noailles, 27 September 1905, *Corr.*, V, 345.

4 Letter to Emile Straus, 3 June 1914, *Corr.*, XIII, 228.

5 Letter to 'un jeune homme', end of June or start of July 1911, *Corr.*, X, 307–8.

6 Céleste Albaret, *Monsieur Proust* (Paris: Robert Laffont, 1973), p. 404.

2. Contexts

1 For an excellent, concise overview of the interplay of 'real' socio-historical context and the people and places of Proust's fiction, see Cynthia Gamble, 'From *Belle Époque* to First World War: The Social Panorama', in Richard Bales, ed., *The Cambridge Companion to Proust* (Cambridge University Press, 2001), pp. 7–24.

2 Much of my historical account here draws on Robert Gildea's excellent *Children of the Revolution: The French 1799–1914* (London: Allen Lane, 2008). See also Charles Sowerwine, *France since 1870: Culture, Politics, Society* (Basingstoke: Palgrave, 2001), Parts I and II.

3 Malcolm Bowie, *Proust among the Stars* (London: HarperCollins, 1998), p. 126.

4 Edmund White, *Proust* (London: Weidenfeld & Nicolson, 1999), p. 83.

5 See *CSB*, pp. 63–9 (66). This article is not included in the English translation.

6 An exploration of the contemporaneous development of the thinking of Proust and Sigmund Freud (1856–1939) is beyond the scope of this chapter. Proust did not read Freud nor Freud Proust but there is, undoubtedly, a good deal of shared ground in their respective conceptions of human behaviour and mental functioning. Interested readers should consult Malcolm Bowie, *Freud, Proust, Lacan: Theory as Fiction* (Cambridge University Press, 1987).

7 Stephen Kern provides a brief, accessible account of these theories in his superb study *The Culture of Time and Space: 1880–1918* (Cambridge, MA and London: Harvard University Press, 2003 [1983]). See pp. 18–19, 135–6.

8 Letter to the Duc de Guiche, 9 or 10 December 1921; *Corr.*, XX, 578.

9 William C. Carter, *Marcel Proust: A Life* (New Haven, CT and London: Yale University Press, 2000), note to p. 69.

10 At the brothel, in his anxiety Proust broke a chamber pot and, as Carter puts it, 'lost his erection and his money'; Carter, *Marcel Proust*, p. 70.

11 Bowie, *Proust among the Stars*, p. 230.

12 He does so in some revealing notes made on Halévy's draft poems; see Anne Borrel, ed., *Marcel Proust: Écrits de jeunesse, 1887–1895* (Paris: Institut Marcel Proust International: Société des Amis de Marcel Proust et des Amis de Combray, 1991), p. 167.

13 See *ASB*, pp. 286–309 (302). 'À propos de Baudelaire', *CSB*, pp. 618–39.

14 Kern, *The Culture of Time and Space*, p. 141.

15 See *Le Banquet* (Geneva: Slatkine Reprints, 1971), p. 5.

16 Henri Bergson, *Matière et mémoire: essai sur la relation du corps à l'esprit* (Paris: Presses Universitaires de France, 1968 [1896]), pp. 26, 144.

17 William James, *Principles of Psychology* (New York: Holt, 1890), I, p. 239, cited by Kern, *The Culture of Time and Space*, p. 24.

18 Walter Benjamin, 'The Image of Proust', in *Illuminations*, trans. by Harry Zohn (London: Pimlico, 1999 [1970]), p. 197.

3.   Early works and late essays

1 See Marcel Proust, *Pleasures and Days*, trans. by Andrew Brown (London: Hesperus, 2004), hereafter *PD*. In French, see Pierre Clarac and Yves Sandre, eds, *Jean Santeuil précédé de Les Plaisirs et les jours* (Paris: Gallimard, 1971), hereafter *PJ*.

2 Letter to Mme Proust, 17 September 1896, *Corr.*, II, 125.

3 Marcel Proust, *Jean Santeuil*, trans. by Gerard Hopkins (Harmondsworth: Penguin, 1985 [London: Weidenfeld & Nicolson, 1955]), 'Introduction', p. 1. This edition is based on Fallois's French text. My French references are to the *Pléiade* edition: Clarac and Sandre, *Jean Santeuil précédé de Les Plaisirs et les jours*, here p. 181. Hereafter references will be abbreviated to *JS* followed by the English then the French page numbers.

4 This essay and 'John Ruskin', the preface to Proust's translation of *The Bible of Amiens*, have recently been republished in the Penguin 'Great Ideas' series: see *Days of Reading*, trans. John Sturrock (London: Penguin, 2008); see also *ASB*, 161–94 and 195–226.

5 Letter to Ramon Fernandez, August 1919, *Corr.*, XVIII, 380.

6 Letter to Robert Dreyfus, 18 March 1908, *Corr.*, VIII, 61.

7 Letter to Louis d'Albufera, 5 or 6 May 1908, *Corr.*, VIII, 112–13.
8 Letters to George de Lauris and to Mme de Noailles, mid December 1908, *Corr.*, VIII, 320–1.
9 Letter to Alfred Vallette, mid August 1909, *Corr.*, IX, 155.

4.   In Search of Lost Time

1 Samuel Beckett, *Proust and Three Dialogues with Georges Duthuit* (London: John Calder, 1987 [1931]), p. 34.
2 The argument of these pages has much in common with the one Proust advances in his essay 'Contre l'obscurité' [Against Obscurity], in which he suggests that contriving to make art complex or obscure is pointless, since the words of everyday language already have an evocative power 'at least as great as [their] power of strict signification': see *ASB*, 137, trans. mod.; *CSB*, 392–3.
3 This is Scott Moncrieff's title; the more recent Penguin translation is much more literal: see *In the Shadow of Young Girls in Flower*, trans. by James Grieve (London: Penguin, 2003).
4 Book-jacket blurb to *The Guermantes Way*, trans. by C. K. Scott Moncrieff and Terence Kilmartin, revised by D. J. Enright (London: Vintage, 1996).
5 See Roland Barthes, 'The Death of the Author', in *Image, Music, Text*, selected essays trans. by Stephen Heath (London: Fontana, 1977); 'La Mort de l'auteur', in *Le bruissement de la langue: Essais critiques IV* (Paris: Seuil, 1984). See Chapter Five for more on Roland Barthes' place in Proust criticism.
6 The divisions in the text between the close of *The Fugitive* and the opening of *Time Regained* differ between the French and English editions. What is printed as the first eight pages of *TR* in English features in the French edition as the closing pages of *AD*. Accordingly, readers of the English text will find the revelations relative to Combray discussed above in *TR*, rather than *F*.

5.   Proust criticism

1 See Leighton Hodson, ed., *Marcel Proust: The Critical Heritage* (1989), p. 75. Full bibliographical details for texts referred to in this chapter are found in 'Further reading'.
2 *The Critical Heritage*, p. 81.
3 See '*La Recherche du temps perdu* de Marcel Proust', in Pierre Nora, ed., *Les Lieux de mémoire* (1984–92), 'Quarto' edition, 3 vols., III 'Les Frances' (1997), pp. 3835–69; *Realms of Memory: The Construction of the French Past*, trans. by Arthur Goldhammer, vol. 2 (1997), pp. 211–45.
4 See William J. Thompson, ed., *French XX Bibliography*, XII, 57–60 (2005–9).

5 Walter Benjamin, 'The Image of Proust' (1929), in *Illuminations*, trans. by Harry Zohn (1999), pp. 197–210 (206, 207).

6 Samuel Beckett, *Proust* (reprinted with *Three Dialogues with Georges Duthuit*, 1987), p. 91.

7 Edmund Wilson, *Axel's Castle: A Study in the Imaginative Literature of 1870–1930* (1979), p. 135.

8 Barthes' essay 'Proust et les noms' [Proust and Names] (1967) is a vital contribution to the study of Proust's attitude to language as well as the style and structuring of the novel.

9 'Roland Barthes contre les idées reçues' (1974), in *Œuvres complètes*, 3 vols., ed., Éric Marty (1994), III, pp. 70–4 (74).

10 Roland Barthes, *Le Plaisir du texte* (1973), p. 22. Readers curious about the place of Proust in Barthes' writing should consult Malcolm Bowie, 'Barthes on Proust', *The Yale Journal of Criticism*, 14 (2001), 513–18 and Anne Simon, 'Marcel Proust par Roland Barthes', in M. Carbone and E. Sparvoli, eds, *Proust et la philosophie aujourd'hui* (Pisa: Edizioni ETS, 2008), pp. 207–21.

11 Jean-Pierre Richard, *Proust et le monde sensible* (Paris: Seuil, 1974), p. 240.

12 Richard, *Le Monde sensible*, p. 263. For an acute assessment of the various positions taken in the criticism of the time with respect to the nature and status of Proust's text, see Florian Pennanech, '*Le Temps retrouvé* et la Nouvelle Critique: le problème de l'achèvement', in Adam Watt, ed., *Le Temps retrouvé Eighty Years After: Critical Essays/Essais critiques* (Bern: Peter Lang, 2009), pp. 239–53.

13 Julia Kristeva, *Le Temps sensible* (Paris: Gallimard 'Folio Essais', 2000), p. 372.

14 Additionally readers of French should consult Anne Simon's *Proust ou le réel retrouvé* [*Proust or the Rediscovered Real*] (2000; new edition 2010), which offers a reading of Proust's conception of reality, aligning it with the phenomenology of Maurice Merleau-Ponty (1908–61).

15 On irony, see Sophie Duval's excellent *L'ironie proustienne: la vision stéréoscopique* (Paris: Honoré Champion, 2004) and on humour, Maya Slater, *Humour in the Works of Proust* (Oxford University Press, 1979).

16 Paul de Man's influential essay 'Reading (Proust)', in his *Allegories of Reading: Figural Language in Rousseau, Nietzsche, Rilke and Proust* (New Haven, CT: Yale University Press, 1979), is an important deconstructive reading of Proust's use of tropes, focusing on what he interprets as the fundamental un-readability of metaphor.

17 See J. M. Cocking, *Proust: Collected Essays on the Writer and his Art* (Cambridge University Press, 1982).

18 See Peter Brooks, *Realist Vision* (New Haven, CT and London: Yale University Press, 2005).

19 See also the essay collection edited by Jean Milly and Rainer Warning, *Marcel Proust: Écrire sans fin* (Paris: CNRS, 1996) and Nathalie Mauriac Dyer, *Proust inachevé: le dossier 'Albertine disparue'* (Paris: Honoré Champion, 2005).

Epilogue: Proustian afterlives

1 These cover 'Combray', 'Swann in Love' (2 vols.) and *Within a Budding Grove* (2 vols.), published in Paris by Delcourt and in English translation by NBM in New York.

2 For an intelligent, critical account of the commodification and 'kitschification' of Proust, see Margaret Gray's chapter 'Proust, narrative and ambivalence in contemporary culture', in her *Postmodern Proust* (Philadelphia: University of Pennsylvania Press, 1992).

3 The Society's web-page (http://pagesperso-orange.fr/marcelproust/sommaire_marcel_proust.htm) includes a complete list of articles and reviews published in their *Bulletin* since its inception in 1950.

4 For an overview of the work of the Équipe Proust, see www.item.ens.fr/index.php?id=13857.

5 A further publication of interest with regard to the present state of Proust studies is *Marcel Proust Aujourd'hui* – a bilingual annual review, first published in 2003, that alternates themed issues with general issues and presents the work of francophone and anglophone scholars on a wide range of topics relating to Proust's life and work.

6 So far Cahiers 54 and 71 have appeared; they are published as a joint venture by the Bibliothèque Nationale de France in Paris and Brepols in Turnhout, Belgium.

7 Harold Pinter, *Remembrance of Things Past*, adapted with Di Trevis (London: Faber, 2000). See also Harold Pinter, *The Proust Screenplay: A la recherche du temps perdu* (London: Faber, 1991).

8 Martine Beugnet and Marion Schmid, *Proust at the Movies* (Aldershot: Ashgate, 2004). Readers of French should also refer to the important collection *Proust et les images, peinture, photographie, cinéma, vidéo* (Presses Universitaires de Rennes, 2003), edited by Jean Cléder et Jean-Pierre Montier.

9 Bennett's play can be found on the double DVD *Alan Bennett at the BBC* (London: BBC Films, 2009) or in print in *A Private Function* (London: Faber, 2004).

10 Alan Bennett, *The Uncommon Reader* (London: Faber, 2007), p. 63.

11 Available on DVD, Roland Petit, *Proust ou les intermittences du cœur* [2007] (Ballet de l'Opéra National de Paris), 2008.

12 For an interview with Cassiers regarding his Proust cycle, see *Marcel Proust Aujourd'hui*, 4 'Proust et le théâtre' (2006), 273–88.

13 Shirley King, *Dining with Marcel Proust: A Practical Guide to the Cuisine of the Belle Époque* (London: Thames & Hudson, 1979; University of Nebraska Press, 2006).

14 See www.pausilippe.com/feuilltonproust.htm for pictures, résumés and travel details.

15 Alain de Botton, *How Proust Can Change Your Life* (London: Picador, 1997).

16 Jonah Lehrer, *Proust was a Neuroscientist* (Boston and New York: Houghton Mifflin, 2007).

17 As Germaine Greer pointed out in a review of the book, although he had many similar anticipatory insights, 'few New Yorkers are going to buy a book called *Montaigne was a Neuroscientist*'. See *New Scientist*, 2631, 24 November 2007.

18 Maryanne Wolf, *Proust and the Squid: The Story and Science of the Reading Brain* (New York: HarperCollins, 2007).

19 Brian Dillon, *Tormented Hope: Nine Hypochondriac Lives* (Dublin: Penguin Ireland, 2009), ch. 7, 'Marcel Proust and Common Sense'.

20 For some brief remarks on Sartre's *Nausea* and other twentieth-century borrowings, see David Ellison, 'Proust and Posterity', in the *Cambridge Companion to Proust*. On Proust's place in the work of two major figures of twentieth-century literature and philosophy, see Mary Bryden and Margaret Topping, eds, *Beckett's Proust/Deleuze's Proust* (Basingstoke: Palgrave Macmillan, 2009); and for a collection of essays which draw connecting lines between Proust and, amongst others, Julien Gracq, Claude Simon and Marguerite Yourcenar, readers should consult *Marcel Proust Aujourd'hui*, 6 'Proust dans la littérature contemporaine' (2008).

21 For instance by Allan Massie in *The Scotsman*, 31 October 2009, whose books section was headed, next to a photograph of Marías, with the question 'Is this man the new Proust?'

22 See, for example, Ian McCall, 'Proust's *A la recherche* as intertext of Makine's *Le Testament français*', *Modern Language Review*, 100 (2005), 971–84.

23 Orhan Pamuk, *The Black Book*, trans. by Maureen Freely (London: Faber, 2006 [1995]), p. 174.

24 Jacqueline Rose, *Albertine* (London: Chatto & Windus, 2001).

25 Kate Taylor, *Madame Proust and the Kosher Kitchen* (London: Vintage, 2003).

26 See Georges Perec et al., *35 Variations sur Proust* (Paris: Le Castor Astral, 2000). Thirty-six years after publishing these 'variations', the *Magazine Littéraire*, in its April 2010 number, ran a special issue on Proust, in part to correspond with a major exhibition at the Musée des lettres et des manuscrits on the boulevard Saint-Germain from April to August 2010.

27 Gray, *Postmodern Proust*, p. 153.

Further reading

The secondary material on Proust is vast. Below are selective lists of important and instructive works, first in English, then in French; available translations of French works are incorporated in the English list.

In English

Biography

Albaret, C., *Monsieur Proust*, trans. by Barbara Bray (New York Review Books, 2003).
Carter, W. C., *Marcel Proust: A Life* (New Haven, CT and London: Yale University Press, 2000).
Caws, M. A., *Marcel Proust* (New York and London: Overlook Duckworth, 2003).
Dillon, B., 'Marcel Proust and Common Sense', in *Tormented Hope: Nine Hypochondriac Lives* (Dublin: Penguin Ireland, 2009), pp. 183–209.
Painter, G., *Marcel Proust*, 2 vols. (London: Chatto & Windus, 1959–65; frequently reprinted).
Tadié, J.- Y., *Marcel Proust: A Biography*, trans. by Euan Cameron (London: Penguin – Viking, 2000).
White, E., *Proust* (London: Weidenfeld & Nicolson, 1999).

Context

Finch, A., 'Despair and Optimism (1913–1944)', in *French Literature: A Cultural History* (Cambridge: Polity, 2010), pp. 120–8.
Gamble, C., 'From *Belle Époque* to First World War: the Social Panorama', in R. Bales, ed., *The Cambridge Companion to Proust* (Cambridge University Press, 2001), pp. 7–24.
Gay, P., *Modernism: The Lure of Heresy from Baudelaire to Beckett and Beyond* (London: Vintage, 2007).
Gildea, R., *Children of the Revolution: The French 1799–1914* (London: Allen Lane, 2008).

Kern, S., *The Culture of Time and Space: 1880–1918* (Cambridge, MA and
    London: Harvard University Press, 2003 [1983]).
Sowerwine, C., *France since 1870: Culture, Politics, Society* (Basingstoke: Palgrave,
    2001).
Zeldin, T., *A History of French Passions: France 1848–1945*, vol. V, *Anxiety and
    Hypocrisy* (Oxford University Press, 1977).

Getting started/reference works

Bales, R., ed., *The Cambridge Companion to Proust* (Cambridge University Press,
    2001).
    Proust 'A la recherche du temps perdu' (London: Grant & Cutler, 1995).
Compagnon, A., 'Marcel Proust's *Remembrance of Things Past*', in Pierre Nora and
    Lawrence D. Kritzman, eds, *Realms of Memory: The Construction of the
    French Past*, trans. by Arthur Goldhammer, vol. 2 (New York: Columbia
    University Press, 1997), pp. 211–45.
Ellison, D., *A Reader's Guide to Proust's 'In Search of Lost Time'* (Cambridge
    University Press, 2010).
Kilmartin, T., *A Guide to Proust* (Harmondsworth: Penguin, 1983); also
    reproduced in the Vintage edition of *Time Regained*.

Early studies and landmarks

Beckett, S., *Proust and Three Dialogues with Georges Duthuit* (London: John
    Calder, 1987 [1931]).
Benjamin, W., 'The Image of Proust', in *Illuminations*, trans. by Harry Zohn, ed.
    by Hannah Arendt (London: Pimlico, 1999 [1970]), pp. 197–210.
Bowie, M., *Proust among the Stars* (London: HarperCollins, 1998).
Compagnon, A., *Proust between Two Centuries*, trans. by Richard E. Goodkin
    (New York: Columbia University Press, 1992).
Deleuze, G., *Proust and Signs*, trans. by Richard Howard (London: Athlone, 2000).
Doubrovsky, S., *Writing and Fantasy in Proust: la place de la madeleine*, trans. by
    Paul and Carol Bové (Lincoln, NE: University of Nebraska Press, 1986).
Kristeva, J., *Time and Sense: Proust and the Experience of Literature*, trans. by
    Ross Guberman (New York: Columbia University Press, 1996).
Wilson, E., 'Marcel Proust', in *Axel's Castle: A Study in the Imaginative Literature
    of 1870–1930* (London: Collins Fontana, 1979 [1931]), pp. 111–54.

General approaches

Bersani, L., *Marcel Proust: The Fictions of Life and of Art* (New York: Oxford
    University Press, 1965).

Carter, W. C., *The Proustian Quest* (New York University Press, 1992).

Finn, M. R., *Proust, the Body and Literary Form* (Cambridge University Press, 1999).

Gray, M., *Postmodern Proust* (Philadelphia, PA: University of Pennsylvania Press, 1992).

Wassenaar, I. P., *Proustian Passions: The Uses of Self-justification for 'A la recherche du temps perdu'* (Oxford University Press, 2000).

Watt, A. A., *Reading in Proust's 'A la recherche': 'le délire de la lecture'* (Oxford University Press, 2009).

Philosophy and fiction

Bowie, M., *Freud, Proust, Lacan: Theory as Fiction* (Cambridge University Press, 1987).

Descombes, V., *Proust: Philosophy of the Novel*, trans. by Catherine Chance Macksey (Stanford University Press, 1992).

Landy, J., *Philosophy as Fiction: Self, Deception and Knowledge in Proust* (New York: Oxford University Press, 2004).

Large, D., *Nietzsche and Proust: A Comparative Study* (Oxford University Press, 2001).

Style and narrative technique

Bowie, M., 'Proust and the Art of Brevity', in R. Bales, ed., *The Cambridge Companion to Proust* (Cambridge University Press, 2001), pp. 216–29.

'Reading Proust between the Lines', in A. Benhaïm, ed., *The Strange M. Proust* (Oxford: Legenda, 2009), pp. 125–34.

De Man, P., 'Reading (Proust)', in *Allegories of Reading: Figural Language in Rousseau, Nietzsche, Rilke and Proust* (New Haven, CT: Yale University Press, 1979), pp. 57–78.

Genette, G., *Narrative Discourse: An Essay in Method*, trans. by Jane E. Lewin (Ithaca, NY: Cornell University Press, 1980).

Graham, V., *The Imagery of Proust* (Oxford: Blackwell, 1966).

Rogers, B. G., *The Narrative Techniques of 'A la recherche du temps perdu'* (Paris: Honoré Champion, 2004), revised and augmented edition of *Proust's Narrative Techniques* (Geneva: Droz, 1965).

'Proust's Narrator', in R. Bales, ed., *The Cambridge Companion to Proust* (Cambridge University Press, 2001), pp. 85–99.

Slater, M., *Humour in the Works of Proust* (Oxford University Press, 1979).

Tadié, J.-Y., *Proust et le roman* (Paris: Gallimard, 1971; reprinted 1986).

Proust and the arts

Beugnet, M. and M. Schmid, *Proust at the Movies* (Aldershot: Ashgate, 2004).
Bales, R., *Proust and the Middle Ages* (Geneva: Droz, 1975).
    'Proust and the Fine Arts', in R. Bales, ed., *The Cambridge Companion to Proust* (Cambridge University Press, 2001), pp. 183–99.
Bowie, M., 'Art', in *Proust among the Stars* (London: HarperCollins, 1998), pp. 68–125.
Brooks, P., 'Modernism and Realism: Joyce, Proust, Woolf', in *Realist Vision* (New Haven, CT and London: Yale University Press, 2005), pp. 198–211.
Cocking, J. M., 'Proust and Music' and 'Proust and Painting', in *Proust: Collected Essays on the Writer and His Art* (Cambridge University Press, 1982), pp. 109–29 and 130–63.
Collier, P., *Proust and Venice* (Cambridge University Press, 1987).
Gamble, C., *Proust as Interpreter of Ruskin: The Seven Lamps of Translation* (Birmingham, AL: Summa Publications, 2002).
Ellison, D., 'Proust and Posterity', in R. Bales, ed., *The Cambridge Companion to Proust* (Cambridge University Press, 2001), pp. 200–15.
Karpeles, E., *Painting in Proust: A Visual Companion to Proust's 'A la recherche du temps perdu'* (London: Thames & Hudson, 2008).
Lehrer, J., *Proust Was a Neuroscientist* (Boston and New York: Houghton Mifflin, 2007).
Nattiez, J.-J., *Proust as Musician*, trans. by Derrick Puffett (Cambridge University Press, 1989).
Prendergast, C., 'Literature, Painting, Metaphor: Matisse/Proust', in *The Triangle of Representation* (New York: Columbia University Press, 2000) pp. 147–59.
Topping, M., 'Photographic Vision(s) in Marcel Proust's and Raoul Ruiz's *Le Temps retrouvé*', in A. Watt, ed., *Le Temps retrouvé Eighty Years After/80 ans après: Critical Essays/Essais critiques* (Bern: Peter Lang, 2009), pp. 309–21.
Tribout-Joseph, S., *Proust and Joyce in Dialogue* (Oxford: Legenda, 2009).

Self, sex and society

Bowie, M., 'Self' and 'Sex', in *Proust among the Stars* (London: HarperCollins, 1998), pp. 1–29 and 209–66.
Cano, C. M., 'Proust and the Wartime Press', in A. Watt, ed., *Le Temps retrouvé Eighty Years After/80 ans après: Critical Essays/Essais critiques* (Bern: Peter Lang, 2009), pp. 133–41.
Carter, W. C., *Proust in Love* (New Haven, CT and London: Yale University Press, 2006).

Eells, E., *Proust's Cup of Tea: Homoeroticism and Victorian Culture* (Aldershot: Ashgate, 2002).

Finch, A., 'Love, Sexuality and Friendship', in R. Bales, ed., *The Cambridge Companion to Proust* (Cambridge University Press, 2001), pp. 168–82.

Girard, R., *Deceit, Desire, and the Novel: Self and Other in Literary Structure*, trans. by Y. Freccero (Baltimore, MD: Johns Hopkins University Press, 1976).

Hughes, E. J., *Marcel Proust: A Study in the Quality of Awareness* (Cambridge University Press, 1983).

'Hierarchies', in A. Watt, ed., *Le Temps retrouvé Eighty Years After/80 ans après: Critical Essays/Essais critiques* (Bern: Peter Lang, 2009), pp. 117–31.

Ladenson, E., *Proust's Lesbianism* (Ithaca, NY and London: Cornell University Press, 1999).

Lejeune, P., 'Écriture et sexualité', *Europe*, 49 (1971), 113–43.

Lucey, M., *Never Say 'I': Sexuality and the First Person in Colette, Gide and Proust* (Durham, NC: Duke University Press, 2006).

Sprinker, M., *History and Ideology: 'A la recherche du temps perdu' and the Third French Republic* (Cambridge University Press, 1994).

Rivers, J. E., *Proust and the Art of Love: The Aesthetics of Sexuality in the Life, Times and Art of Marcel Proust* (New York: Columbia University Press, 1981).

Terdiman, R., *The Dialectics of Isolation: Self and Society in the French Novel from the Realists to Proust* (New Haven, CT: Yale University Press, 1976).

Wilson, E., *Sexuality and the Reading Encounter: Identity and Desire in Proust, Duras, Tournier and Cixous* (Oxford University Press, 1996).

Critical reception and genetic criticism

Bowie, M., 'Barthes on Proust', *The Yale Journal of Criticism*, 14 (2001), 513–18.

Cano, C. M., *Proust's Deadline* (Urbana, IL: University of Illinois Press, 2006).

Hodson, L., ed., *Marcel Proust: The Critical Heritage* (London: Routledge, 1989).

Pugh, A., *The Birth of 'A la recherche du temps perdu'* (Lexington, KY: French Forum Publishers, 1987).

The Growth of 'A la recherche du temps perdu': A Chronological Examination of Proust's Manuscripts from 1909 to 1914, 2 vols. (University of Toronto Press, 2004).

Schmid, M., 'The Birth and Development of *A la recherche du temps perdu*', in R. Bales, ed., *The Cambridge Companion to Proust* (Cambridge University Press, 2001), pp. 58–73.

Winton (Finch), A., *Proust's Additions: The Making of 'A la recherche du temps perdu'*, 2 vols. (Cambridge University Press, 1977).

Edited volumes

Benhaïm, A., ed., *The Strange M. Proust* (Oxford: Legenda, 2009).
Bryden, M. and M. Topping, eds, *Beckett's Proust/Deleuze's Proust* (Basingstoke: Palgrave Macmillan, 2009).
Kotin, A. and K. Kolb, eds, *Proust in Perspective: Visions and Revisions* (Urbana, IL: University of Illinois Press, 2002).
Watt, A. A., ed., *Le Temps retrouvé Eighty Years After/80 ans après: Critical Essays/ Essais critiques* (Bern: Peter Lang, 2009).

In French

Place of publication is Paris unless stated otherwise.

Biography

Albaret, C., *Monsieur Proust* (Robert Laffont, 1973).
Tadié, J.-Y., *Marcel Proust: Biographie* (Gallimard, 1996).

Getting started/reference works

Bouillaguet, A. and B. G. Rogers, eds, *Dictionnaire Marcel Proust* (Honoré Champion, 2004).
Compagnon, A., 'La *Recherche du temps perdu* de Marcel Proust', in Pierre Nora, ed., *Les Lieux de mémoire* [1984–92], 'Quarto' edition, 3 vols., III 'Les Frances' (Gallimard, 1997), pp. 3835–69.
Laget, T., *L'ABCdaire de Proust* (Flammarion, 1998).

Early studies and landmarks

Barthes, R., 'Proust et les noms', in *Le Degré zéro de l'écriture suivi de Nouveaux essais critiques* (Seuil, 1972 [1967]), pp. 121–34.
Compagnon, A., *Proust entre deux siècles* (Seuil, 1989).
Deleuze, G., *Proust et les signes* (Presses Universitaires de France, 1964; 4th edn, rev. 1970).
Doubrovsky, S., *La place de la madeleine: écriture et fantasme chez Proust* (Mercure de France, 1974).
Kristeva, J., *Le Temps sensible: Proust et l'expérience littéraire* (Gallimard 'Folio Essais', 2000 [1994]).
Richard, J.-P., *Proust et le monde sensible* (Seuil, 1974).

General approaches

Tadié, J.-Y., *Proust: le dossier* (Belfond, 1983; various reprints).
    Proust: la cathédrale du temps (Gallimard 'Découverte', 1999).

Philosophy and fiction

Barthes, R., *Le Plaisir du texte* (Seuil, 1973).
    'Roland Barthes contre les idées reçues' [1974], in *Œuvres complètes*, 3 vols.,
        ed. Éric Marty (Seuil, 1994), III, pp. 70–4.
Carbone, M. and E. Sparvoli, eds, *Proust et la philosophie aujourd'hui*
        (Pisa: Edizioni ETS, 2008).
Descombes, V., *Proust: philosophie du roman* (Minuit, 1987).
Simon, A., *Proust ou le réel retrouvé* (Presses Universitaires de France, 2000; new
        edition, Honoré Champion, 2010).

Style and narrative technique

Duval, S., *L'ironie proustienne: La vision stéréoscopique* (Honoré Champion, 2004).
Genette, G., 'Proust palimpseste', in *Figures I* (Seuil, 1966), pp. 39–67.
    'Proust et le langage indirect', in *Figures II* (Seuil, 1969), pp. 223–94.
    'Métonymie chez Proust', in *Figures III* (Seuil, 1972), pp. 41–63.
    'Discours du récit', in *Figures III* (Seuil, 1972), pp. 65–282.
Milly, J., *Proust et le style* (Lettres modernes, 1970).
    La Phrase de Proust: des phrases de Bergotte aux phrases de Vinteuil
        (Larousse, 1975; reprinted 1983).
Spitzer, L., 'Le style de Marcel Proust', in *Études de style* (NRF, 1970 [German
        edition 1961]).
Tadié, J.-Y., *Proust et le roman* (Gallimard, 1971; reprinted 1986).

Proust and the arts

Azérad, H., *L'univers constellé de Proust, Joyce et Faulkner: le concept d'épiphanie
        dans l'esthétique du modernisme* (Bern: Peter Lang, 2002).
Bedriomo, E., *Proust, Wagner et la coïncidence des arts* (Editions Place, 1984).
Bouillaguet, A., *Marcel Proust: le jeu intertextuel* (Editions du Titre, 1990).
Butor, M., *Les œuvres d'art imaginaires chez Proust* (London: Athlone Press, 1964).
Jullien, D., *Proust et ses modèles: les 'Mille et Une Nuits' et les 'Mémoires' de Saint-
        Simon* (José Corti, 1989).
Marcel Proust Aujourd'hui, 6 'Proust dans la littérature contemporaine' (2008).
Nattiez, J.-J., *Proust musicien* (Christian Bourgois, 1984).
Tadié, J.-Y., ed., *Marcel Proust: l'écriture et les arts* (Gallimard/Bibliothèque
        Nationale de France/Réunion des musées nationaux, 1999).

Self, sex and society

Dubois, J., *Pour Albertine: Proust et le sens du social* (Seuil, 1997).
Girard, R., *Mensonge romantique et vérité romanesque* (Grasset, 1961).
Hughes, E. J., 'La représentation du monde social dans *Combray*', in *Marcel Proust Aujourd'hui*, 3 (2005), 63–80.
Lejeune, P., 'Écriture et sexualité', *Europe*, 49 (1971), 113–43.
Sakamoto, H., 'La guerre, l'art et le patriotisme', in A. Watt, ed., *Le Temps retrouvé Eighty Years After/80 ans après: Critical Essays/Essais critiques* (Bern: Peter Lang, 2009), pp. 142–53.

Critical reception and genetic criticism

Mauriac Dyer, N., *Proust inachevé: Le dossier 'Albertine disparue'* (Honoré Champion, 2005).
Milly, J. and R. Warning, *Marcel Proust: Écrire sans fin* (CNRS, 1996).
Pennanech, F., '*Le Temps retrouvé* et la Nouvelle Critique: le problème de l'achèvement', in A. Watt, ed., *Le Temps retrouvé Eighty Years After/80 ans après: Critical Essays/Essais critiques* (Bern: Peter Lang, 2009), pp. 239–53.
Simon, A., 'Marcel Proust par Roland Barthes', in M. Carbone and E. Sparvoli, eds, *Proust et la philosophie aujourd'hui* (Pisa: Edizioni ETS, 2008), pp. 207–21.

Edited volumes

Cléder, J. and J.-P. Montier, eds, *Proust et les images, peinture, photographie, cinéma, vidéo* (Presses Universitaires de Rennes, 2003).
Compagnon, A., ed., *Proust, la mémoire et la littérature* (Odile Jacob, 2009).
Watt, A. ed., *Le Temps retrouvé Eighty Years After/80 ans après: Critical Essays/ Essais critiques* (Bern: Peter Lang, 2009).

Index

Cambridge Introductions to Literature

Authors

Margaret Atwood *Heidi Macpherson*
Jane Austen *Janet Todd*
Samuel Beckett *Ronan McDonald*
Walter Benjamin *David Ferris*
Chekhov *James N. Loehlin*
J. M. Coetzee *Dominic Head*
Samuel Taylor Coleridge *John Worthen*
Joseph Conrad *John Peters*
Jacques Derrida *Leslie Hill*
Charles Dickens *Jon Mee*
Emily Dickinson *Wendy Martin*
George Eliot *Nancy Henry*
T. S. Eliot *John Xiros Cooper*
William Faulkner *Theresa M. Towner*
F. Scott Fitzgerald *Kirk Curnutt*
Michel Foucault *Lisa Downing*
Robert Frost *Robert Faggen*
Nathaniel Hawthorne *Leland S. Person*
Zora Neale Hurston *Lovalerie King*
James Joyce *Eric Bulson*
Thomas Mann *Todd Kontje*

Herman Melville *Kevin J. Hayes*
Sylvia Plath *Jo Gill*
Edgar Allan Poe *Benjamin F. Fisher*
Ezra Pound *Ira Nadel*
Marcel Proust *Adam Watt*
Jean Rhys *Elaine Savory*
Edward Saïd *Conor McCarthy*
Shakespeare *Emma Smith*
Shakespeare's Comedies *Penny Gay*
Shakespeare's History Plays *Warren Chernaik*
Shakespeare's Poetry *Michael Schoenfeldt*
Shakespeare's Tragedies *Janette Dillon*
Harriet Beecher Stowe *Sarah Robbins*
Mark Twain *Peter Messent*
Edith Wharton *Pamela Knights*
Walt Whitman *M. Jimmie Killingsworth*
Virginia Woolf *Jane Goldman*
William Wordsworth *Emma Mason*
W. B. Yeats *David Holdeman*

Topics

The American Short Story *Martin Scofield*
Comedy *Eric Weitz*
Creative Writing *David Morley*
Early English Theatre *Janette Dillon*
English Theatre, 1660–1900 *Peter Thomson*
Francophone Literature *Patrick Corcoran*
Literature and the Environment *Timothy Clark*

Modern British Theatre *Simon Shepherd*
Modern Irish Poetry *Justin Quinn*
Modernism *Pericles Lewis*
Narrative (second edition) *H. Porter Abbott*
The Nineteenth-Century American Novel *Gregg Crane*
The Novel *Marina MacKay*
Old Norse Sagas *Margaret Clunies Ross*
Postcolonial Literatures *C. L. Innes*